LOUISE WREN The
Little Red
Patient

The true story of Maddie, a disabled fox cub who
learned to live with humans

MEREO
Cirencester

Mereo Books

1A The Wool Market Dyer Street Cirencester Gloucestershire GL7 2PR
An imprint of Memoirs Publishing www.mereobooks.com

The Little Red Patient: 978-1-86151-451-6

First published in Great Britain in 2015
by Mereo Books, an imprint of Memoirs Publishing

The address for Memoirs Publishing Group Limited can be found at
www.memoirspublishing.com

The Memoirs Publishing Group Ltd Reg. No. 7834348

The Memoirs Publishing Group supports both The Forest Stewardship Council® (FSC®) and
the PEFC® leading international forest-certification organisations. Our books carrying both the
FSC label and the PEFC® and are printed on FSC®-certified paper. FSC® is the only
forest-certification scheme supported by the leading environmental organisations including
Greenpeace. Our paper procurement policy can be found at
www.memoirspublishing.com/environment

Typeset in 11/17pt Goudy
by Wiltshire Associates Publisher Services Ltd. Printed and bound in Great Britain by
Printondemand-Worldwide, Peterborough PE2 6XD

CONTENTS

Dedication

Acknowledgements

Introduction

FOR ANGIE AND CHRISTIAN, WITH LOVE

ACKNOWLEDGEMENTS

My grateful thanks to: Paula Robinson in Australia for putting me in contact with Angie Evans; Mary Page, for her poem; Maggie Bruce, for several superb photographs (photos of Foxes and Maybe More); vet Harry Evans; and all fox lovers and friends who followed 'Maddie updates' and photos on Facebook and encouraged me to write this story.

Thank you National Fox Welfare Society, for the information on Toxoplasmosis.

Thank you Martin O'Sullivan for the title and to editor Chris Newton for sorting out the mess I made when I sent him the wrong version of the manuscript.

My biggest thanks go to Angie and Christian, who gave a little disabled fox cub a chance of life and who kept me up to date with news and photographs.

All photos are mine except where stated otherwise.

Some names and places have been changed to protect anonymity.

INTRODUCTION

When I went out for dinner one night, I did not expect to come home with a fox. But that's life - unpredictable, shocking, surprising. Yet again, my close encounter with a fox has been an ongoing education, and I am ever more convinced that every animal on earth deserves a fair deal.

In this story, which may be considered controversial by those people who believe that 'nature should not be interfered with' and 'wild is wild', you will meet not only a disabled fox cub and rescued wild and tamed foxes, but also tame-bred pet foxes, whose existence I was not even aware of. They are very beautiful and varied in colour and can make lovely and unusual pets. I have included information and advice on owning a pet fox as I feel it is important to know that owning one is not a decision to be taken lightly; it is a lifelong commitment. Their life-span is about 14 years, and they are expensive to keep.

CHAPTER 1

"That's not a squirrel!"

We shall never know what happened to the little fox cub before I found it crawling in the gutter of a busy road one night. We can only speculate.

It was twenty-five minutes past eleven on April 28th 2014, a dark, chilly and damp Monday night, and I was driving home from a meal out with my friend Madelon at a nearby pub about six miles from my home in Surrey. Madelon had come to visit me from Holland and was staying with me. It had been a terrific night with delicious food and a great deal of laughter, but how quickly events and moods can change in life.

I knew that on the way home there were some roadworks which I was keen to avoid by taking a different route. However, because we were chatting, I took a wrong turning.

'Aw no', I sighed as soon as I turned off, really annoyed with myself, 'I didn't mean to take this road. Oh well, never mind, I know where I'm going.'

I carried on along that road. All of a sudden, not a hundred yards from where I had taken the wrong turning, my headlights picked out a small animal in the gutter on the left. It was moving, and during the few seconds it was in view I had the impression it was trying to climb back up onto the kerb of the footpath. I say *trying* because its back legs did not seem to be co-operating; somehow they seemed lame, and it looked as if it could not push itself up onto the kerb to get to the cover of the long grass and shrubs beyond.

I could not see the animal clearly when I passed it, but it was definitely struggling to get up onto the path even though the kerb was not particularly high. It was frantically shuffling and crawling in the gutter, and I thought perhaps it was a squirrel that had been run over.

Deciding to investigate, in case it needed help, I did an emergency stop, managing not to stall the car, which was a miracle in itself as I had not performed one for years. With the hazard warning lights on and watching for approaching traffic, I slowly reversed the car a little way, trying to get back to the little road casualty I believed I had spotted. There were no street lights, it was pitch black along that road and I needed some light to investigate properly.

Madelon cried out in alarm 'what are you doing?' She did not understand why I had suddenly stopped and started reversing.

'I've seen an animal by the side of the road,' I said. 'It can't get up onto the kerb, it must have been hit by a car, but it's still alive. It looks like it's a squirrel. I can't leave it there, I'm going to pick it up.'

'And what on earth are you going to do with it?' she asked.

'I'm going to take it home and phone the wildlife rescue people. They have a 24-hour ambulance rescue service, they'll come and get it'.

I drove back a little further to the spot where I thought I had seen the animal, I stopped and got out. At the same time, Madelon opened the passenger door and I heard her say, 'Hey, it's not a squirrel, I think it's a small fox cub!'

My heart nearly stopped in shock. 'No! Not a fox cub?' I exclaimed.

'Yes, yes, I'm sure it is a small fox cub,' she repeated.

People who know me will also know how much I love foxes. I am quite obsessed by them, boring everyone to death talking about them and helping to raise money for fox charities. Furthermore, six weeks earlier, my book about another fox, Foxyloxy, had just been published and I was on a high.

'Oh yes, I'm certain it's a fox cub and it's tiny,' Madelon repeated.

I opened the boot, grabbed the blanket I always keep in there and slowly walked towards the area where I believed I had seen the animal. It was very dark, but then a little way ahead, I suddenly saw it bathed in the lights of the car. It was about ten feet in front of me, still trying to get up onto that kerb and, oh dear god yes, it *was* a fox cub, a really, really small one. In fact it was the smallest one I had ever seen. What a shock! My heart started racing.

Other cars were whizzing past now and the little cub was obviously very scared. It was scrabbling about in the gutter, and when I slowly approached, it tried to get away from me; it just could not move very fast. I dropped the blanket around it and lifted it very gently, covering its eyes as I had seen many wildlife rescuers do on TV. I noticed a little streak of blood by the side of its mouth, but apart from that, at first glance, it did not seem to have any other visible wounds or injuries – perhaps it had just been struck a glancing blow and was simply shocked and bruised. It did not struggle or make a noise when I picked it up.

I decided to take it home and ask for some advice from the local wildlife rescue centre. It was so very small, and still quite downy as well, although there was some red fur showing on its face and flanks; it had the typical white tip to the end of its tiny tail. It looked perfect. I gave it to Madelon to hold and got back in the car, as I thought it was best to get some help as soon as possible.

I was extremely upset and shaking as I drove home and I must have asked several times if it was still alive, as I know how easily wild animals can die just from shock. Madelon was holding it on her lap in the blanket and peeked in; its eyes were open, its ears flat against its head. It was not moving at all now.

As soon as we got home I tried to remember where the phone number for the wildlife rescue organisation was. I could not find it; why wasn't it in my address book? I was getting flustered, but I suddenly remembered that it was in my mobile phone - for emergencies, of course. Yes, I was certain it was in my phone, but in the panic I could not find my phone either and I could not remember my mobile number to dial the phone to locate it, although in normal circumstances I know the number off by heart.

I spotted my *Little Red Thief* book on the arm of the sofa. 'The book!' I spluttered. 'The addresses and phone numbers of the rescue centres are in the back.'

Madelon found the phone number and with the cub in the blanket on my lap and me shaking like a leaf I made the phone call to the nearest wildlife rescue centre, only to get an answering machine. How frustrating! I tried to leave my name, address and phone number, but in the panic of the moment I was a bit slow and the message time ran out. I dialled once more and decided to leave my landline number and ask for a call back - and then I could not remember my own phone number either. Good grief, what a state to get in to, talk about shock! At work as a midwife I had always been so calm when an emergency arose, but now that I had retired and was dealing with an unfamiliar scenario I was losing the plot, or so it seemed.

Finally I got the number right and asked them to call me back as soon as possible. It was now just past midnight.

While I was waiting for a reply, I peeled back the blanket and looked at the cub. It seemed rigid and lifeless and had closed its eyes. Had it died? I put my hand on its chest, trying to feel for a heartbeat. The cub was quite cool to the touch; I could not feel anything, and although I have a stethoscope I did not have a clue where it was.

All of a sudden the cub opened one eye. Oh, thank goodness, what a relief, it was still alive! It looked exquisite, so tiny yet so perfect. It was just showing a little bit of orange fur on its face and flanks, with white fur along the sides of its mouth where I had seen the tiny streak of blood on the left hand side. It had long black front 'socks' and short black 'ankle socks' on its back legs, and with its little black ears and dark brown downy areas it was just beautiful. It had a little round tummy and felt very soft and downy to the touch. Its legs were no thicker than my index finger, and there appeared to be a thin oily mark on its back approximately one inch long in the fur just above the start of the tail. The back legs and tail appeared limp, although Madelon said she had seen them move a little and I also thought I had seen them moving as it was trying to crawl away from me on the road.

I gently stroked the cub's ears and spoke to it very softly. It did not move or react to the sound of my voice or to my touch, so I covered it up again, still holding it on my lap. I did not touch it in any other way as I did not want to hurt it, so I did not know if it was a male or a female. All the time we had kept the lights in the room quite low, as I did not want to stress it any further; we were still waiting for the phone to ring.

I decided to put it in my cat carrier basket to keep it safe. It was raining quite heavily when Madelon set out with the torch to the garden shed to fetch the basket; she put some clean newspapers in it whilst we waited. I examined the cub's body again, keeping its eyes covered so as not to traumatise it. It remained motionless on my lap and still felt quite cold. I wondered how long it had been on the road. There were definitely no external injuries or visible deformities.

It seemed ages before the phone rang and I was able to tell the wildlife rescuer that I had found a small fox cub on the road. The first thing he asked me was: 'what colour is it?' which seemed to me to be a very silly question indeed, because I had told him it was a fox.

'It's a red fox cub' I replied.

'Yes, but what colour is it?' he insisted.

Of course I realised then that this was not such a silly question after all, because you can roughly determine the age of a cub by its colouring. They are born covered in dark brown furry down, which gradually changes to the orangey-red of a grown-up fox. I described the colour of the cub to him, adding that it still had some down. He seemed to think it was 'quite well on'. I told him that, from the colour, it looked about six weeks old, but that it was very small, and that it had no visible wounds or injuries.

He asked if it could move its legs. I looked at Madelon and she nodded, so I said 'yes, I think so'.

'Oh good, it could have been a spinal injury' he said. 'Just keep it warm and dry and give it some water and dog food. Then, if it has recovered by the morning, you can just release it where you found it.'

I was surprised. 'Are you not going to come and pick it up?' I stammered.

'No, there's nothing we would do overnight and in any case you're not doing anything different from what we would do here. Give us a ring in the morning if there is a problem.'

Somewhat surprised, I thanked him for his advice and put the phone down. I suddenly seemed to have a fox cub in the family.

I did as I was told and also took two photographs of it - for the record - then put the cub in the cat carrier, blanket and all, with two little dishes at one end of the cage, one with water and one with some dog food. I covered the cage with a fleece and put it on the dining room table; I even put the heating back on as it seemed a bit chilly in the room. It was well past midnight by now so the heating had been off, and I wanted to make sure it was nice and warm downstairs.

The adrenaline was still flowing, so Madelon and I had some tea and biscuits, as neither of us could even think of going to sleep; we were just too shaken by the night's turn of events. The cub was awfully quiet and we wondered if it would survive the night. Both of us were convinced it would not.

All of a sudden, I had a thought - when people have had a shock, a cup of sweet tea is a well-known remedy. So I went to the kitchen and made half a slice of bread and honey, cut it up into tiny pieces and slid it into the cage on top of the dog food. I do know that foxes have a very sweet tooth and I just thought it might help. The cub was half hidden by the blanket, so I did not investigate any further.

As I was still wide awake, I put a message on Facebook to say that I had found a tiny fox cub on the road after taking a wrong turning on the way home. I mentioned that it was possible it had been run over but that it was safe and warm at my house and that we were taking advice from a wildlife rescue organisation.

It never fails to amaze me how many people are still up and logged on to the internet after 1 am. In normal circumstances I am in bed by 11.30 pm, midnight at the latest. Friends and acquaintances, many of whom had read the story of *The Little Red Thief* and knew how much I care for foxes, could not believe that I had been the one to find that cub and talked about fate. They are enchanting animals as far as I am concerned and I had found a little fox cub. I could hardly believe it myself.

About an hour and a couple of mugs of tea later I suddenly heard some faint clicking noises coming from the carrier. What on earth was going on now? I had a peek under the cover and could just make out the cub's face: it was still lying down, but it was shivering and its teeth were chattering, hence the clicking noises, but unquestionably it was alive. Poor little thing, it must have been terrified at finding itself alone, hurt and contained in a box in strange surroundings. I covered the basket over again and, fearing the worst, went to bed about 2 am. What a night it had turned out to be.

I certainly did not expect to sleep, but I did and I was in a deep sleep when at around 4 am my cat, Molly, jumped onto the bed. She seemed very agitated: walking all over me non-stop, meowing and making odd, yowling noises, something she never normally did. Wide awake suddenly, I could not ignore Molly. I stroked her, and she calmed down. Then I heard it – the most pitiful crying downstairs. In the middle of the night it sounded quite loud as well and it was not the sort of whining noise a puppy would make. It was a kind of hoarse, screeching crying, I think Molly had been saying 'Excuse me, have you any idea what is going on downstairs? Do you know what's on your dining room table? There's a fox in the house!'

I immediately realised the noises had to come from the cub, and although it worried me very much to hear it wailing like that, I had been told by Wildlife Rescue to leave it in peace, so I refrained from going downstairs to investigate. At least the crying proved that it was still alive. I have not forgiven myself for that yet, because it was not until days later that it occurred to me the cub might have been calling and crying for its mother – how very sad. With hindsight, I should have ignored the advice to leave it alone and gone downstairs to give it a cuddle - poor little thing.

Many rescue organisations believe that you should never cuddle fox cubs, even when bottle-feeding orphans, and I know for a fact that tiny cubs have been taken away from fosterers for fear of them becoming imprinted because they were cuddled or kissed the way a puppy or kitten would have been. Just how exactly these rescue organisations expect you to bottle-feed a cub without any human contact is beyond my comprehension. I now believe it would be unkind not to and I know I am not the only one to think this.

I quote Martin Hemmington, founder of the National Fox Welfare Society (NFWS):

'Foxes are sociable animals and to take this contact away from an orphaned cub is cruel. When cubs are feeding from the mother she will lick and tend to them, again and again to have a happy cub drinking, and thus this contact is very important in rearing her litter during the early days. Once they get to a certain age cubs become neophobic - they fear anything new. When they integrate with other cubs later on, you are soon forgotten. So if a cub was crying out for companionship I would hold it close to my chest until it calmed down; a cuddle, I believe, is as essential as a bottle of milk.'

That makes much more sense to me and I will know better in the future. It was not as if the cub I had found had any siblings to cuddle up with for comfort.

I lay in bed wide awake, wondering what could have happened to the cub that night. Could it have been the runt of the litter, unceremoniously dumped at the edge of the vixen's territory because she had no use for it? Fox mothers always know when one of their cubs is 'not quite right'. Had it been attacked by another animal? Had it got left behind when the vixen had moved her cubs from one den to another? Or had it just got lost whilst exploring and had it been trying to get back to its family when it had crossed the road and as a consequence had it been struck by a car? All of these scenarios played through my head as I lay in bed listening to its pitiful cries.

The cub cried on and off for over an hour and then, all of a sudden, it stopped. I wondered if it had died at that point and I tortured myself with that thought until at last I dozed off again, waking with a start at regular intervals during the rest of the night.

CHAPTER 2

Difficult decisions

At 7.30 am I was wide awake again, and this time I did not hesitate to go downstairs. It was very quiet when I entered the room and I was afraid to look into the cage for fear of what I would find. I made a cup of tea before looking under the fleece that covered the cage.

When I peered inside, the smell that hit me made me wince. The cub was alive all right. It looked at me suspiciously from where it was, huddled in a corner. There was dog food all over the cage and the blanket, and everything was wet as a result of the water bowl having been tipped up. Amongst it all there were two perfectly-shaped blobs of black faeces. This, I decided, was a good sign: clearly its bowels and bladder were working as they should, and there was no sign of blood anywhere, indicating that there were no internal injuries.

The cub looked wet and dirty and seemed absolutely terrified. The ears were back and flat against its head, its eyes big and round – a sure sign of stress. It was pressed up against the far corner of the carrier, sitting up, but with the lower part of its body slung to one side. There was no sign of the bread with honey on it and, looking at the amount of dog food strewn around the cage, I guessed that the bread was probably all the cub had eaten overnight.

In order to put clean bedding in I decided I would take the cub out of the messy carrier, so I opened the door and reached in. However the docile and quiet little cub from the night before immediately started hissing and spitting, and bit me. There's gratitude for you! Its little needle-like teeth had pierced the skin of my thumb, and I was bleeding. Undeterred, I decided to put my gardening gloves on.

At this moment Madelon came downstairs. 'Is it still alive?' she asked, sounding surprised.

'Yes, and it has just bitten me. I wanted to change the bedding as it's all dirty.' I mentioned the crying in the night, but she had not heard a thing. I took a couple of photographs and then we implemented Plan B: I would grab the cub and Madelon would clean the box. This time I opened the carrier from the top in order to grab it by the scruff of its neck, saying 'less of your nonsense now, I am trying to help you, this is what your mother would do'.

The cub went limp, as they do when you scruff them; I lifted it out without any problems and sat it on a towel on my lap. I could see its back legs were just hanging down. They seemed no thicker than my index finger. The cub was quite grubby underneath with bits of leaves, mud and dog food sticking to its belly and hind legs, and although I could not see it clearly I thought it was a male.

'It's a little boy, Madelon!', I called out to the kitchen. 'If it had been a girl I would have called her Maddie, after you. Now it will have to be Eddie.'

'Oh, shame!' she laughed, and began to clean and disinfect the carrier.

The cub sat quite calmly on my lap; I stroked his velvety little black ears, which were pricking up now, and talked softly to him. He was nice and warm and sat very still. I admired his exquisite colouring, his beautiful clear eyes, so full of life, his cute black whiskers and the two sooty stripes either side of his face and I fell in love with him straight away. He was so perfect and so vulnerable, just a little baby. Whoever had struck him on the road or run him over had not even stopped and had just left him to struggle, eventually to die. It was a heart-breaking thought, although of course they may not have known they had hit him.

At a quarter past nine, I rang the wildlife rescue people again. It was a strange conversation; they had no record of my call or my conversation with the rescuer from the previous night, which I found odd. I asked what they would do with an injured fox cub that could not use its back legs. What if it could not be rehabilitated and returned to the wild? How long would they give it to recover?

There was only one answer: if it could not be rehabilitated to go back to the wild, they would put it down. There was no choice. The person at the end of the line did not ask if I wanted to speak to a member of the vet team for further advice; she said the cub should just be put back where it was found and then left, 'for nature to take its course'.

I was flabbergasted, to say the least. What? Put it down, my pretty little cub? I was determined to find an alternative solution and seek a second opinion.

I put the phone down, very disillusioned with their rescue service and their advice. In my experience, many wildlife rescue organisations can be quite fanatical about returning animals to the wild and do not always consider alternative options; many of them say they struggle for funds and are staffed by volunteers, so they don't always have the time or the money for costly vet fees or treatments. There are some admirable exceptions that I know of: the National Fox Welfare Society, The Fox Man at Freshfields Animal Rescue, which both have a 24-hour ambulance service, to name but a couple, but I know there are many more who will try and find permanent homes in sanctuaries for foxes that cannot be returned to the wild for one reason or another. Other rescues have a strict mantra that 'wild is wild'; meaning if they even just think it cannot be returned to the wild it will be put to sleep. Unfortunately my local one belongs to the latter, hence my reluctance to hand Eddie over to them.

It was only nine hours since we had found Eddie and I was not convinced that he had got over the shock yet. I decided to give him another day of rest here to see what would happen and to consider the way forward. I did not want to take him to the local wildlife hospital, as I did not trust them to give him the best chance. That might have been doing them an injustice, but there we have it. On social media such as Facebook and TV we read about many success stories; we see photographs and videos of amazing rescues and recoveries which encourage people to support the charity by donating money, but we do not often hear about it when foxes are brought in and are then euthanized quite rapidly, given up as hopeless cases. They will not keep or treat them in hospital for long for fear of imprinting. Unquestionably some foxes *are* hopeless cases when they are either very sick or have horrendous injuries, when it is only right to end their suffering. I am not so naive as to think we can save every fox that is found sick or injured, but I truly believed that they would not have given Eddie much time if they thought his legs were lame; I thought they would just take one look at him and then say 'sorry, he did not make it' when I enquired after him a couple of days later.

This was confirmed when I spoke with the director of another rescue organisation. He said they would give him a week to recover, ten days at the most, and if he was no better by then, he would be put to sleep. Would there be any other treatment or therapy maybe? He found my question laughable. 'Perish the thought, we don't do that, maybe just a course of anti-inflammatories'.

I was convinced Eddie's spine was not broken. I saw no deformities or injuries to his legs or back, but I thought he could have bruising and swelling affecting his movement, and toyed with the idea of taking him to my own vet to ask his opinion. However, not every vet is willing to treat wildlife and Eddie might have been handed over to the RSPCA or the other local wildlife rescue after all. Eddie did not seem to be in pain as I was holding him on my lap and he did not wince or cry out when I touched him. Yes, I *am* aware that most animals hide pain well but even so...

I gave Eddie a cuddle and put some clean water and food in the carrier plus a quarter of a jammy doughnut for a sweet treat. I covered him over again to keep him in the dark to rest and recover from the shock until I had found a satisfactory solution or a vet willing to take a look at him. After all, it had been only a few hours since we had found Eddie. Madelon and I had some breakfast and got ready to go out for lunch as this was the last day of her holiday in England. When we returned home later that afternoon, we felt the same anxiety as we had that morning, would Eddie still be alive?

With some trepidation I removed the cover from the cage; he was indeed alive and still sitting in the corner the same way we had left him; he had not touched his food or his doughnut. I checked the Facebook page where I had put the news of his rescue the night before and discovered that I had been inundated with messages; unsurprisingly not all of them agreeing with my course of action, ie taking him home and resting him. One heartless person even suggested I should have reversed the car over him to end his suffering; another said I should have left him for the magpies or other predators to eat, and yet others called me cruel and evil for keeping him caged and prolonging his suffering.

I was even threatened with an investigation by the animal rights people and accused of keeping him only because I wanted photos for a book. A book? Get real! When I see an animal that has been hurt my first thought is certainly not 'oh good, now I can write a story about it'. Nothing had been further from my mind, and I wondered if people had read my post properly. I did mention that we were taking advice from the wildlife rescue organisations and that they had been unwilling to come and collect him at midnight so I was just resting him for the day to recover from the trauma. I did not want to put him back where I had found him in the state he was in, and I did not want him to be put down so quickly. I knew full well that I could not keep him, as I had no facilities or expertise in looking after fox cubs. I just have my medical background to fall back on. He was not suffering, had no visible injuries and he had only been here for about 14 hours by now; he was safe and warm and I was still considering the way forward.

Many more people were very positive and supportive

and thought he deserved a chance; they said he was lucky to have been found by me. Others lectured me about 'not interfering with nature', 'imprinting' - a favourite word with many wildlife rescuers - and 'letting nature take its course'. Everyone had an opinion, and everyone told me what to do. When you love foxes you certainly learn who your friends are - you also get to take a lot of stick.

Then a breakthrough: a message on Facebook from a nice lady called Angie Evans-Smith, which read: 'Do not let them put him down, I will have him and we will cope. I have two other rescued foxes and we have a massive outdoor enclosure to keep the foxes safe; one of our other foxes was lame when we rescued it and now it can walk. We will know how to look after him - I am married to a vet'. Angie had been alerted to my news by her friend, Paula, in Australia.

Well, that was the breakthrough I had been waiting for. I made up my mind there and then to give Eddie to Mrs Evans-Smith. After all, where there's life there's hope, and it is my belief that every living creature deserves a chance of life, whatever form that life may take, as long as there is no suffering. It seemed an ideal solution to me, so I contacted her.

Her home was a long way from me in the north east of England and, as it was late afternoon, I had no chance of taking Eddie up there that day. We discussed how best to get him to her house the next day. Clearly there was an element of urgency about getting some help now. Angie had already stated that she could not pick him up as she could not leave her other foxes for more than three hours; I realised a round trip would take much longer. There was an added problem in that I had to take Madelon to the station the next day to get the train to Gatwick as she was going home, so I would not be free until about 2 pm.

I decided that once I was free I would drive him to Cambridgeshire myself; this meant Eddie would be staying with me another night. He seemed very quiet and settled, so we just left him in peace after checking that he had food and water and that his bedding was dry.

I did not hear him at all that night and once again, I experienced a feeling of acute anxiety as I came downstairs the next morning. Would he still be alive? I carefully lifted the cover of the basket only to find Eddie looking at me distrustfully; he was in a complete mess, just as he had been the previous morning. He seemed to have eaten a few bits of food and was sitting in the corner clutching the soft toy dog. His ears were still back against his head and his eyes were still big and round, so yes, he was stressed, but he looked very much alive to me, if rather grubby, and he also seemed much more alert.

I ran a bowl of warm water and lined the scales with some kitchen roll. Then I carefully picked him up out of the cage by the scruff of his neck and dipped his filthy rear end and legs into the warm water, moving him very gently around. He did not struggle at all, and when the dirt was off him I could see that he definitely had no wounds anywhere; maybe that little oily patch on his back, but nothing else.

His tail and back legs were still hanging limp and there was no reaction when I gently squeezed his toes as Angie had asked me to do. Clearly he could not feel anything, poor little boy. I weighed him; he was 850 grams, less than two pounds, very small for a cub which I had estimated at six weeks on the basis of his colouring. I wondered again if he had sustained some bruising and swelling that would account for the lameness, but I knew that he would be examined thoroughly by a vet later that day, and possibly have X-rays, so I did not pull him around at all.

This time Madelon put the gloves on and held him on her lap as I cleaned and disinfected his cage and took some more photos of him; we just held him gently, stroking his ears and talking softly to him. After a while he did not seem quite so stressed, his ears were up and not back or flat down like they had been previously that morning and he was looking around.

A couple of my friends even popped in to have a look at this latest, if temporary, addition to my animal family. He did not seem to be the least bit frightened and they were astonished at his beauty and size. I put some photos on Facebook and said he was going to a vet's family in Cambridgeshire just as soon as I had taken Madelon to the station. There were many messages of support and requests for future 'Eddie updates'. Most people loved seeing him and were glad he had not been put to sleep and that he would have the company of other foxes.

I blocked those people who said I was just prolonging his suffering and those whose comments were abusive or negative, as I was not going to get into any discussions or so-called debates about such matters. I had made my decision, and that was that. I know everyone is entitled to their opinion, but there is no need to be so personally abusive and insulting. Fanatic animal rights people were the worst - you would not think they had the best interests of an animal at heart. Yes, I know the ideal place for a wild fox is in the wild, but he looked full of life, he was not visibly damaged as such and I thought he ought to be given a chance of life and not to be left to die in the wild, as he obviously could not fend for himself, being unable to walk. If he recovered quickly I could always get him back and release him.

I am fully aware of that famous adage 'don't interfere with nature', but tell me, are hunting, culling, trapping and shooting or gassing animals not interfering with nature? Is intensive farming of animals, injecting growth hormones and antibiotics not interfering? Is the use of pesticides not interfering? Is it natural to take a calf away from its mother soon after its birth so *we* can drink the milk? Have you heard a mother cow crying for its newborn baby which now has to be raised on artificial food? Is that natural? Is rearing game birds only to be shot for so-called sport natural? Is fur-farming natural? Not to mention, trophy hunting, poaching and killing animals for the fur trade or so-called medicines. I will let you think about all that and draw your own conclusions. All I know is that animals deserve better. The cruelty we humans inflict on animals on a daily basis is a world-wide disgrace and the damage we do to their natural habitat and, as a result the planet, is a real threat to its continued existence.

These are controversial issues, but I had made my decision with regards to this precious injured cub.

CHAPTER 3

The long road to safety

At about two-thirty pm on Wednesday 29th of April, thirty-eight hours after I had found the cub, I set out for the M25 and the route north. If you are not familiar with the M25 orbital around London, let me tell you that it resembles a car park most days. From where I live, southwest of London, I have to travel clockwise past Heathrow airport - a nightmare at the best of times. I had planned my route carefully and had taken some water and wipes for the journey, which had been estimated as two and a half hours for the one hundred and thirty miles by the online route planner. Eddie was clean and looked comfortable; he had his cuddly toy dog, food and water. In the car the cage, covered with a dark towel, had been strapped securely on to the passenger seat next to me; that way I would be able to keep an eye on him.

After three hours of driving I was nowhere near my destination and needed a break. I pulled into a service station parking the car in the shade and opening all windows and doors so we could have some fresh air. The weather was unexpectedly warm that afternoon, so it was hot in the car and I worried about my little passenger. Every now and then Eddie looked as if he was sleeping, but basically he had not moved since leaving home.

After approximately half an hour's break, we continued our journey north. The traffic proved to be horrendous; it had increased even as it was nearly five o'clock by now - rush hour! Combined with roadworks and diversions, it was very slow going. I phoned Angie to let her know I was delayed but that I was definitely on my way. I did not want her to think that I was not coming. She said she had everything ready for Eddie, large cage, vet bed and special food, as well as sandwiches, cakes and coffee for me. The landscape was quite flat with yellow rape fields on both sides of the road as I was getting nearer to my destination. I encountered even more traffic and diversions, got lost, and had to phone for instructions again. What a nightmare drive, and all the time I was worrying about Eddie.

You will have gathered by now that I do not have satnav in my car, and that the map, which I thought was in the boot, was nowhere to be seen.

It was half past seven when I finally arrived at Angie's house. It had taken me five hours to get there, twice as long as estimated. I was met at the gates by Angie's son Christian and Angie herself. I cannot tell you how relieved I was. Once inside I took Eddie out of the cage and placed him gently in Christian's arms. From the way he was holding the cub and cradling it in his hands, I could immediately see that this was a very caring and sensitive young man. I told them that Eddie had not eaten or drunk anything that day as far as I knew. Angie looked at him and straightaway said 'He is never six weeks, more like four and a half or five weeks. He's so tiny, but I suppose he could be the runt of a litter. He needs some milk'.

Later she told me that her first thoughts had been: *This little tiny fox cub, looking with such round frightened eyes and ears held down which I know means he is stressed - warm goat's milk will start to calm him down and hopefully he will go to sleep. I know we have a real challenge before us, I just hope we can help him. Oh, what a sweet little fox cub, we have not had a little boy fox before. I do hope you make it, little one.*

I wondered how they were going to make him drink the milk, but as I have already mentioned, they have experience in caring for foxes. Christian went to warm some goat's milk for Eddie and mixed it with some soft veterinary food (so-called a/d food) which is especially formulated for animals who are recovering from surgery, accidents or trauma. Christian held Eddie and Angie held a spoon with some of the warm, milky mixture to the side of his mouth. To my utter amazement he started to lap from the spoon, and once he tasted it he had more; he must have been starving. Then he licked his paws. What a beautiful sight. Angie also thought he had curled his toes around her finger whilst she fed him.

She then gently wiped him underneath and to my great surprise she said 'Did you think this was a boy? Look, it is a little girl'. Oh dear, they had never had a little boy fox before, which I know they would have liked, and now they still did not have one, but clearly she was right, Eddie was a little girl. How embarrassing! I used to be a midwife and had not known the difference. Mind you, I had already told you that I did not move him around too much. How was I going to confess this on the Facebook pages, where everyone was waiting for an 'Eddie' update? Now she was going to be 'Maddie' after all, I but decided to leave it at Eddie for a bit and to tell them later. I asked Angie and Christian to keep the name 'Maddie', and they agreed. So Maddie she was from then on.

In the meantime, Maddie, quiet and cradled in Christian's arms, fell asleep against his chest. She must have been exhausted. Carefully, he put her in the cage on a soft fleecy vet bed and left her to sleep. How tiny and vulnerable she looked in that huge cage with the big cuddly toy dog next to her. She needed to recover from the trauma of the accident and the journey. The plan was that Christian would sleep in the room downstairs with her and that he would look after her during the night. Angie's vet husband,

Harry, would examine her in the morning, as he was still working and was not at home.

Before darkness fell we went outside to meet the ponies, Billy and Blue, also rescues. When called they came over from the far end of their field and I was able to stroke their soft noses. I was also shown the external fox enclosure, which was in the process of being enlarged by Christian. This would give the foxes masses of extra room outside. It still rather resembled a building site, yet I could already see what it was going to be like and how large it was going to be. It would be very spacious with sleeping accommodation, kennels to hide in and connecting doors and gates to the current fox enclosure and to the house. It would definitely be big enough for three foxes.

CHAPTER 4

Scarlett and Darla

Inside again now, Maddie was still asleep and, as we chatted over coffee, sandwiches and cake, they told me about the other foxes residing with them: Scarlett, a rescued wild red fox, and a tame bred silver fox called Darla. Wow, what a beauty she was! Silver foxes are basically black with longer silver hairs in their coat. I had never seen a silver fox before. They used to be wild in the UK, and are a natural variety of the red fox, but they were hunted to extinction for their exquisite fur - how horrifying. After 200 years of breeding the foxes for their fur here, a breeding programme was initiated in Russia in 1959 to see if foxes could be pets. The most placid ones having been selected, these silver foxes are now quite tame. There are a handful of breeders of exotic animals in England, but I had never heard of anyone here in the UK having a pet fox. In the course of the year and through online groups I have now met several pet fox owners in the UK and also in Australia and the USA. I will tell you more about pet foxes later, but first, more about the two resident foxes that I met that night.

Christian brought Scarlett in to meet me; she had been a very young red fox cub about three weeks old when she came to live with them. She was their first fox, although they had many other animals, most of them rescues. The people who had found her on the road did not know how to look after her, so she had been handed in to the vet's surgery after forty-eight hours. Scarlett had also been lame when she was found, although not to the same degree as Maddie and for a different reason. Nonetheless, Angie and Christian had managed to rear her successfully. Now one year old, she was a beautiful red vixen that had completely recovered. Clearly she could not go back to the wild as she was too tame, having been hand-reared. She regarded me with distrust, as she does not like strangers very much, but she seemed perfectly at ease with Christian and his mother. She had a magnificent white-tipped tail, and as much as I wanted to, I did not touch her.

When Scarlett was first given to Angie she was only tiny, so she asked for advice from a wildlife rescue organisation. All they told her was to hand the cub over to them; however, they were a six-hour drive away in the south, and Angie declined. So she trawled the internet for information. Fortunately, a friend who owned a pet fox saw her plight and gave her advice; so did the Pet Fox Owner's website. Her friend told her how much to feed Scarlett, to treat the cub like a kitten and to try her with a litter tray; they followed his advice, and from day one Scarlett used a litter tray. How amazing! However, she would not eat or drink if they did not hold her so she was spoon fed till she was big enough to eat and drink by herself. Yes, spoon fed rather than fed by syringe as there is less chance of choking. Fox cubs generally start to feed themselves from about 6-7 weeks, which is when they would get weaned in the wild.

Scarlett was such a good baby, loving, playful and very funny. She slept in Christian's room on his bed and loved playing there with him. When her legs were stronger and he moved his hand under the duvet she would perform a perfect foxy pounce, just as a cat would chase a mouse and pounce on it. When she was eleven weeks old the family acquired a Golden Doodle puppy of the same age, Oscar, to keep her company. The animals became great friends and romped and played together all the time. They are still friends to this day.

To his dismay, when Scarlett was four months old, she began marking Christian's bedroom as *her* territory, and she started to wet and scent on the carpet; this had to be removed and lino was put down instead to enable easier cleaning. Still, all was going quite well until she was about six months old when she became a teenage fox and this sweet, playful, lovable cub started to behave like a Tasmanian devil. She became very destructive. She bit a huge hole in Christian's duvet, completely destroyed his armchair, chewed through various leads, ripped wallpaper off and scratched the paintwork as she went about her foxy business. She stole his cordless computer mouse and chewed his leather wallet, as well as the upholstery on the sofas in the lounge. She hissed at and nipped Christian and Angie, who were at a loss to understand what had happened to their sweet little fox cub. They blamed themselves, and thought that they had done something wrong.

August 2013 was hot, and a portable air-conditioning unit had been put upstairs. Scarlett watched as Christian pushed the digital buttons and decided that she could do this too, so she learned to push the buttons. Foxes are extremely inquisitive and curious, not to mention intelligent, and I have since heard from other fox owners that their foxes also seem to love technology.

Apart from all the damage, Christian must have had many sleepless nights, as Scarlett was semi-nocturnal, going to sleep for a few hours initially, then keeping him awake by scratching and making noises before falling asleep again in the early hours of the morning. He told me that he had been semi-suicidal by the time she was six months old. It was time for action.

They found out through the Pet Foxes website that she

needed to go and live outside and have her own space, so Christian decided to build an outdoor enclosure for her at the back of the house just off the kitchen. For a guy with a law degree but no experience in construction, this must have been a tremendous challenge. However, with a bit of advice he learned how to mix concrete and how to lay the concrete floor which would stop Scarlett digging her way out and any wild foxes from digging their way in. He erected metal fencing all around, covering the top with wire and securing it firmly so Scarlett would not be able to escape. The whole area was built around a tree, which was left in the middle of it all for added interest.

In the meantime, with his own room practically in ruins, Christian decided to move permanently downstairs with Scarlett. He put a bed in the room just off a very large downstairs bathroom, which in a previous life had been a bedroom with a small conservatory. This conservatory had been taken down and turned into a room with a sliding door to the outside. They put lino on the floor, for obvious reasons. Via the now en suite bathroom there was access to the hall and the rest of the house. In his new room Christian fixed his TV high on the wall, and then made a custom-built desk for his computer with a hole in the plasterboard for ventilation, a 'fox proof' top and all the leads boxed in. He added a large cage with her bed in it to keep Scarlett from mischief at night.

During the day, Scarlett was carried through the house

to her outside pen, which was 4m x 4m in size, or approximately 13 feet square in old money. A large kennel lined with straw and an empty barrel on its side had been placed in this enclosure for shelter; foxes like to climb, and love to have places to hide in, giving them a bit of privacy every now and then.

Inside the house, Scarlett continued systematically to demolish the family's belongings. Curtains were pulled off their rails and ripped up, the wallpaper was scratched off the walls and paint was stripped from the doors. She ripped the upholstery on the arms of the chairs and sofas in the living room, chewed and tore at the underside of the sofas and, when there were visitors, she messed on the carpet in excitement. Shoes, especially rubber Crocs, were trashed - usually when people were wearing them. She was a little vandal. Although she nipped, she never gave a nasty bite, but can you imagine the damage in the house? If you are at all houseproud, you would definitely not want a wild fox as a pet.

Scarlett also stole Angie's iPad and then put up a right old fight when she tried to get it back. She tried playing games on it too. One game she particularly liked was 'Insects'; she loved chasing the bugs across the screen. In fact, she loved anything with buttons, such as remote controls and mobile phones, and it earned her the nickname 'Techno Fox'. You may wonder why Scarlett was still allowed in the house, but once a fox has stolen your heart there is no way back – they are magical.

One day, the family went out, leaving Scarlett at home in Christian's room. When they returned they were baffled as to why the house and garden were in complete darkness. Fortunately there was a modern fuse box in the house, so the lights were soon on again. They started to investigate what could have occurred. At first glance there appeared to be nothing amiss; it was a mystery. They looked around all the rooms, but there seemed to be no problem. Finally, in Christian' downstairs room, they spotted a small piece of electrical cable hanging from the ceiling where the light fitting had been. Using it as a ladder, Scarlett had climbed up on top of her cage, and ripped the light fitting right off the ceiling, thereby blowing the electrics. Can you believe it? If it hadn't been for that modern fuse box, she could have been killed. There have not been any electric light fittings in that room since, as it is currently Darla's residence.

Another day they went to the local garden centre with Christian carrying Scarlett; he told me there was no point putting a harness and lead on her as she would only have wrecked it straight away. He had not even realised she had shredded his shirt until someone noticed that he was covered in scratches and, pointing at Scarlett, asked 'Are they vicious?' Well no, not really, Scarlett was just a teenager, and after Angie mentioned her behaviour on the Pet Fox Owners' website a fox owner replied 'do you mean to say you don't know about the *crazies*?' This person explained what happened to 'teenage' foxes in their first year, and then Angie understood why Scarlett behaved as she did.

I don't think many people know about this period in a fox cub's life, certainly not in the UK, as we tend not to have foxes as pets here. Certainly I had never heard of it, so it came as a revelation to me too - and I believe to a couple of wildlife rescue organisations as well.

Additionally, this website recommended that Scarlett should be spayed, as this seemed to calm foxes down. It would also prevent her breeding, should she ever manage to escape. It would appear that her hormones had a lot to answer for, just as in human teenagers.

When she was taken to the surgery in the car, she sat on Christian's lap and was promptly car sick. Once there, she made a fuss, hissing and nipping and then took an instant dislike to the vet - she has never liked him since. Christian says 'she hates him'. Scarlett was always more frightened of men than of women - she still is. Christian is the exception of course, as he is her 'daddy'; she really bonded with him when she was little. She was a member of the family, and like a puppy she had been vaccinated, wormed and micro-chipped.

At this point let me explain a little bit about those 'Crazies' as they call it on the Pet Foxes website, I quote from their page:

'During a cub's first autumn – usually in October, but it can be as early as August or as late as November- they go through a series of temperament changes. These changes are temporary, but very dramatic. The cub becomes aggressive, fearful, hyperactive, destructive, nippy and prone to frustrated tantrums. It will seem as if you have lost all progress with them, but it is important to remember that this is only a temporary phase. You may feel like you have done something horribly wrong in raising your cub, or be worried that there is something terribly wrong with them, or think that you are not cut out to keep a fox. Do not worry, this is a normal part of your cub's development and it only happens the first year. So what causes these Crazies? In the wild, this is the time that your cub would be driven away by its parents to fend for itself. Other foxes, meanwhile, have no desire to let these young intruders into their territory, so they attack and drive off the newcomers. The cubs have to struggle to establish their own territory and fend for themselves. Their hormones kick into high gear, so at the same time they are fighting to carve out a place in the world, they are dealing with internal chemistry they have never had before. The fear and aggression that you see in your pet is a remnant of this - they are afraid that you, as their surrogate 'parent', are going to attack them and drive them away. The key to surviving the Crazies is to stay consistent with your training, to be patient and, above all, to remember that this is only a phase. By the time your cub reaches one year of age, but usually considerably earlier, it will have settled back into being a reasonable animal again. The hormonal effects die down as the fox gets more used to them, and they start to believe that you are not going to bite them and chase them away. It will be hard to believe that the temperamental monster you had in October is the sweet cub you have curled up in your lap in January.'

Apparently the above passage applies to all foxes, be they wild or tame-bred.

Just before Christmas 2013 there was another fox addition to the Evans family when 'Darla' arrived. Darla was a tame-bred silver fox. She had been one of two pet foxes, but after one died she was on her own and miserable; not much was known about her history. Her owners gave her up and Angie took her in.

She was around seven months old when she arrived, the same age as Scarlett, and it was hoped she and Scarlett would be friends. As predicted, Scarlett's teenage behaviour was beginning to settle down and she was a great deal calmer. They never experienced Darla's crazies, as she probably had already been through that period by the time she came to them; Christian told me that she only ever chewed one wire. Remember that Darla was a pet fox and tame-bred, not a wild fox like Scarlett.

The arrival of Darla brought its own problems though. At first she could not be with Scarlett at night because they did not know how the foxes would behave together, so they had to be in separate cages which were linked; they could still see each other though. Moreover, Darla was not familiar with her new human family and they did not know her; she was anxious and bit them when they carried her to the outside pen. Therefore a decision was made to build a bigger enclosure off Christian and Scarlett's downstairs room with a connecting door to the first enclosure. This meant that the foxes would have a huge outside area and could be separated if necessary, also they would not need to be carried to and fro.

Before returning home that night, I met Darla, a stunningly beautiful silver fox; she had a fine-looking coat and was bigger than Scarlett. Had she not had the typical white tip to her tail I would have thought she was a small wolf.

After moving the rest of the food out of the way, as he tends to be a bit of a hoover, Oscar the Golden Doodle came in to say hello too. My goodness, what an enormous dog. He was a giant, the size of a large long-legged sheep, with a huge head and wild curly fur. Apparently he had not stopped growing yet either, as he was only one year old. What's more, his size did not stop him from trying to sit on my lap, which was very funny; he just about got his two front paws on and towered above me. Maddie slept through it all and the other animals took no notice of her in the cage.

Scarlett and Darla mainly live in the outside enclosures these days, but are also allowed in the house from time to time. Christian believes that as well as pets they should be allowed to be semi-wild and do their own thing – a happy medium. Scarlett and Oscar are still best friends and there is a great video on YouTube where you can see all of them playing outside together: it's called *Scarlett the Fox Cub*. **www.youtube.com/watch?v=QttAtfpkiL0**

Having read Scarlett's story, I would now like you to imagine what Christian must have thought when I turned up at their house with yet another wild red fox cub. If I remember correctly I think he had thought 'oh no, here we go again'.

CHAPTER 5

Nightmare journey

It was 10 pm by now and time for me to go home. After being reassured by Angie that I could come back any time to visit Maddie, and could even bring my grandchildren to see her, I reluctantly set out for the journey back home. I was not sure when I would see her again, I did not think I could face that five hour-journey again in a hurry, but Angie said that I could perhaps get a lift with a friend of hers who was coming in a couple of weeks' time from London to visit them. That sounded like a great idea. I felt quite emotional leaving little Maddie behind, and I was wondering if I had done the right thing.

I was tired and it had been my intention to stay the night at a local Travelodge which I had seen on the way up, about 15 miles away, but the moment I left the house, the heavens opened and the rain came down by the bucketload, lashing horizontally on to the windscreen. I could barely see the dark unlit road, even with the headlights on, let alone the road signs, and I crawled along at 10mph, peering into the darkness, the windscreen wipers doing overtime and the car windows misting up fast.

I appeared to be travelling on a dyke, the sides of which fell away very steeply to deep ditches on both sides; I really did not want to end up in one of those. It was a serious cloudburst, it was pitch black and it was terrifying. As a consequence I missed the turning to the main road and found myself hopelessly lost, unable to find the main road and therefore unable to find the A1 home. The few road signs I managed to see meant nothing to me, the road numbers and village names were unfamiliar, so I carried on in the direction I *thought* was south until I ended up in a bigger town called Wisbech. I had no idea where that was.

Wisbech resembled a ghost town in the darkness. It seemed completely deserted and I had to drive around the one-way system a couple of times before I spotted a man walking his dog. When I asked for directions to London, he laughed and said I was not far from Kings Lynn in Norfolk. Norfolk? Yes, it turned out that I was well on my way further north. I could not believe it; I was absolutely going the wrong way and had been going around in circles for over an hour - so much for my orientation.

He gave me directions and finally, about eleven-thirty pm, I spotted a sign for London; it was quite obvious by then that I was way past that Travelodge. I did not know what to do; it had been such a long day and I was feeling stressed and tired. That was when I noticed there was absolutely no traffic on the A1. Also the rain had ceased, so I pulled myself together and decided to drive home, stopping at the first service station I came across to fill up with petrol and buy some sweets and water to keep me going. I told myself that it would not be the first time I had arrived home late and that I could do it. In any case, had I stayed the night I would have had to drive home in the Monday morning traffic going south towards London – surely that would have been worse?

During the long drive home I felt really tearful; I fretted about Maddie and asked myself again if I had done the right thing. Undeniably she was in good hands, but I could not stop feeling as if I had abandoned her. Images of her tiny little figure huddled with the toy dog in the corner of that big cage kept flashing through my mind, poor little baby. The last forty-eight hours and all its events had really affected me.

With no other traffic on the road, I made good progress and to raise my spirits further the M25 was also quite clear, with very few cars; it was one-thirty am by now and I seemed to be the only one on the road. I finally arrived home at half past two in the morning. I must have broken the speed limit a few times, but fortunately I have not had any tickets sent to me yet. Before I crawled into bed I left Angie a message to say I had driven home after getting lost and not finding the Travelodge.

CHAPTER 6

Intensive care

Angie phoned me the next afternoon to tell me that Maddie was alive and well; she had been bathed and had eaten her breakfast of goat's milk, vet food and a bit of ham. What a relief! She was still fed with a spoon, as she did not want to eat by herself.

Christian, however, had not had a very peaceful night; he had slept on the floor next to her cage and had woken up when he 'felt something move on the floor next to him'. Somehow Maddie had got out of the cage; she must have climbed to the top and dragged herself from there onto the floor, as there was no other way out. It defied belief that this tiny cub with her lame back legs could have done that. He'd had a real job catching her again as well. I could not believe what I was hearing. That cage was huge, about 3 feet tall and 4 feet long, and she had climbed out of it? The top must have been loose for her to squeeze through it as well. No one had expected her to be able to climb at all and I was swiftly assured that this would not happen again - the top of the cage was now securely fixed. She had also been crying in the night, but had settled down after some more food and cuddles.

I asked if she had been seen by Harry, the vet. Yes, he had seen her, and I was right; there did not seem to be anything broken and she was not in any pain. Her bowels and bladder were working normally, which ruled out a broken spine, however her back legs were still not moving. She was too small and too traumatised to be anaesthetised for X-rays so soon; they would have to wait for her to be a bit stronger first.

I asked about the blood by her mouth and the vet thought that she had bitten her tongue during the accident – if indeed it had been a car accident; after all, we could not be sure what had happened to the poor little mite. Angie promised to keep in touch and she was as good as her word, sending me messages nearly every day, and also a couple of photos of Maddie in her bath - the washing-up bowl - Maddie being dried with a big fluffy towel and Maddie having her food fed to her from a spoon. It was very reassuring to talk to Angie and see the photos, but I so wished I could have been there for her.

During the following days Maddie was wormed, treated for fleas and had some little ticks removed. Whilst she was in the warm bath water, Christian massaged her legs, moving them gently up and down to improve the circulation. He gave her a bath and hydrotherapy every day, which she did not particularly like. Her ears would go flat, showing her displeasure, but at least she did not bite him. At first she had her hydrotherapy bath twice a day as, like all babies, she used to wet herself and they did not want her to get sore. When she was held afterwards they put a nappy underneath her, a tiny one - like one you would use on a premature baby, she was that small.

In her cage she had a litter tray. Because Maddie would not have been able to climb over the edge of a normal litter tray, they fashioned a tray for her out of the kind you use with a paint roller, as they have a sloping edge – I thought this was inspired. Maddie used her litter tray with varying degrees of success. After her bath she used to have her breakfast and then she slept again in the cage in the living room on her vet bed, cuddling her teddy. That way she was safe; she did not move very much anyway.

Christian carried on building the new enclosure when she was asleep. With three foxes now, a larger outside space became somewhat urgent. Obviously Maddie could not mix with the bigger foxes or any of the other animals there, as she was too small and had not been vaccinated yet. Furthermore they might have attacked her, as she was so tiny and vulnerable, although as a rule foxes are very caring towards cubs. Christian carried the little patient around inside his fleece when he went about his business during the day and when he was working on his computer in the evening she was on his lap, so she was not alone. He really wanted her to bond with him as this would make it easier to look after her and hopefully help her recovery. Fox cubs usually bond with their main carer, so he not only fed and bathed her, he played a great deal with her, resulting in strong bond with him: he had to be the one to hold her whilst Angie fed her, and if or when the roles were reversed, little Maddie was not happy, expressing her displeasure by hissing at Angie, can you believe it? She was such a cheeky little madam.

I asked if Maddie was eating well. 'Oh yes, she has her special goat's milk mixture, with ham, cheese or chicken, and she likes yoghurt and watermelon'; she usually buries her cheese under her blanket to eat later and tips up her water bowl every night. She is always given some food to eat during the night including a tomato'.

Whilst at first Maddie needed to be persuaded to eat and needed to be fed, it was not long before she started lapping her milk from a little ramekin. The first time she did this, Angie videoed it for me. You can see it at **www.youtube.com/watch?v=dnPXxlkTN9A**. I could hear that looking after her in those early days required two people.

In his spare time, when Maddie was asleep, Christian was busy building that new outside enclosure so that there would be a larger play area for the three foxes. This extension would be linked to Christian' downstairs room via the existing sliding door so that the foxes could shelter inside, in case the weather was bad. In addition there would be a connecting door between the existing enclosure and this new one, so that the wild red foxes and the tame Darla could be separated if necessary. It was hoped that the two wild red foxes would eventually be friends.

One day Angie carried Maddie outside to meet Scarlett, but the feisty little madam just hissed at the big fox. She was fascinated however by the two ponies in the field, and during the following days she also made friends with Archie, a little West Highland terrier who had arrived as an anniversary present on the same day that Angie picked up puppy Oscar. Oh yes, I have not mentioned yet that the family owned seven dogs in total as well as a rescued macaw, 'Mac', a handful of rescued chickens, the two ponies and five cats.

I updated my Nature Watch group page on Facebook nearly every day with 'Eddie updates', which were eagerly awaited by many people, and I finally confessed to everyone that Eddie was a girl and was now called 'Maddie'. How people laughed at my mistake! Well, most did, but some ridiculed me, saying that I claimed to be a fox expert and had not even known what it was. Had I been a fox expert I would have looked after her myself, but I was not, which was the reason for taking her to Angie, to get expert care with vet supervision.

The internet trolls kept making an appearance too, accusing and abusing and *demanding* to see X-rays; in the end I just blocked them all, flatly refusing to debate or even discuss my decision to have this cub looked after privately. It was infuriating, especially as most of them had not even read the original post.

I am of the opinion that every living creature should be given a reasonable chance of life, whatever form of life that may take, as long as there is no suffering, an opinion not shared by everyone. Unsurprisingly, I did not tell anyone where Maddie was staying; just stating that she was with a vet's family 'up north'. The abuse really took off when I mentioned that – should Maddie not ever be able to walk – they could get some wheels for her, the same way that we have seen wheels for disabled dogs work, thereby enabling Maddie to enjoy the large garden.

I am doing an injustice here to the many lovely people who wrote to me and offered to help pay for her care and her wheels or anything else she might need. They could not have been more supportive if they had tried and I was very grateful. However, Angie would not accept anything and said that they could manage. They did not have sanctuary status, and it would be unethical to accept money. It would remain a private arrangement. Despite this, one lovely lady sent me twenty pounds in the post anyway, and I spent it on chicken, treats and toys; others made donations to fox charities.

A few days later, on May 5th, I went to a 'Wildlife Rocks' event in Guildford. It was a marvellous day and I met some lovely people. The highlight that day was meeting Brian May – yes, the man himself, lead guitarist of Queen. A huge conservationist and wildlife rescuer, he works hard to save the lives of badgers and foxes, and if possible he returns them to the wild or gives them sanctuary.

I was lucky enough to have a few private words with him. I told him about Maddie and asked him what he would have done. 'The same as you - thank you', he said and shook my hand. Oh, he made me feel so much better about not having her put down. I just knew I had done the right thing and I told everyone on Facebook what he had said.

As he is a member of Queen, Maddie's fans reckoned we now had 'royal' approval and decided Maddie was a princess. When I jokingly replied that I had better go out to buy her a tiara then, a couple of people thought I was serious and told me how 'cruel and undignified' that was for a fox that *should be out in the wild*. How they could possibly think I was really going to buy her a tiara was beyond me. Dear oh dear!

During April half-term, my grandson, Marcus, set up a FB page for my book 'The Little Red Thief' and I thought it might be better to put any further Maddie updates on there and on my own page instead of in the group. It was a shame for those fans who were really interested in her progress but it stopped the trolls, the arguing and the debating in the Nature Watch group as to the rights and wrongs of keeping a wild injured fox alive, which was a relief. Anyone who asked after Maddie was directed to these other pages where they would be able to find her updates. It is now May 2015 and the page has over 2000 'likes'. Maddie's photos are shared around the globe, from America to Europe and Japan to Australia – she has become world famous and her fans finally persuaded me to write down her story.

CHAPTER 7

A foxy convention

I was so looking forward to seeing Maddie the week after the Wildlife Rocks event. I could not wait, because the good bit of news was that Angie thought she had seen her curl her toes; furthermore, three days before my visit I was told that her little legs were beginning to move and that she could even hold them up. However, she was still flat on the ground when she moved. At least she was trying, what a trooper. It gave us all hope.

I wondered if she would recognise me, a bit optimistic perhaps but you never know. Call me crazy, but I decided to wear the same jumper and perfume I had been wearing when I rescued her. She might know me by my smell - after all, it had only been ten days and foxes are renowned for their sense of smell.

Even though I heard nearly every day how she was doing, I could not wait to see Maddie again, and it was arranged with Angie's friends that I would meet them in London and they would give me a lift, which was very kind. Accordingly, twelve days after I had found Maddie I travelled to London to meet Angie's friends. They picked me up at Finchley tube station so we could travel up together, saving me the horrendous car journey on my own.

Nothing could have prepared me for what happened next. Just before I got into their car, they opened the boot, saying 'we have a surprise for you'. They reached in and retrieved a cat carrying basket; I peered inside but was not sure what I was looking at. There on the towels rested a tiny black animal. It did not look like a kitten, more like a puppy, and like a twit I asked: 'what is it?'

They explained that it was a silver fox cub, five weeks old, and Angie had bought him as a companion for Maddie, to stimulate her and keep her company so she wouldn't be lonely. That did it! I promptly burst into tears, I was speechless. My little Maddie would have a foxy friend of a similar age - two to three weeks younger actually. How very thoughtful. Fox cubs should have company, it's unnatural for them to be on their own.

'Would you like him on the back seat with you?' they asked.

'Yes, of course'.

'You can touch him or have him on your lap, he is used to being handled because he is tame bred.'

We set out on the journey and I gently took the cub on my lap on a towel, I could now see the white tip of his tail. It was definitely a fox cub and he was slightly smaller, darker and more downy than Maddie. How very precious. I was told he was five weeks old, which seemed a very young age to be taken away from his mother, but apparently tame foxes need to bond with their new human owners as soon as possible. By feeding a cub that young the bond will be stronger, therefore they will be easier to handle when they grow up. I never even knew you could get tame fox cubs in the UK.

During the trip I heard how Angie had seen him and his brother on Facebook, and had thought they were in America. Then somebody had told her, 'No, they are not in America they are in Kent'. So she had bought him as a companion for Maddie in order to stimulate her. Her friend had picked him up the day before we travelled up there. I realised that I had also seen that same picture on Facebook - 'two little black fox cubs looking for a good home' - and assuming they were in America, I had paid no further attention to the post. No reason why I would even consider getting a pet fox.

The little black cub sat on my lap and dozed on and off all the way there. We only stopped once, to change the wet towel he sat on for a dry one and to feed him some finely-chopped cooked chicken. I held him close and stroked his soft, downy black fur; he was perfect of course, and not so different from a tiny puppy. When we arrived at the house they all laughed, as I was still feeling all emotional at this big surprise. Honestly, my love of foxes has turned me into an emotional wreck!

Another of our Facebook friends, Maggie, had been invited to this foxy 'convention' as well; she has many wild foxes living in her garden, which is even further north than Angie's house, and she takes the most marvellous photographs of them all. You simply must look at her FB page 'Photos of Foxes and maybe More'. We all trooped inside; there were six of us all together.

It was such an exhilarating afternoon. Angie had laid on an excellent buffet of sandwiches and cream cakes and after we had a coffee, we opened a bottle of champagne and drank a toast to the new babies - as you do. Maddie was in her cage in the room and Christian took her out for me to hold. He gave me a tiny nappy for her to sit on and because I was not sure how she would react, I sat on the floor with her on my lap next to Maggie, who was holding the new cub on her lap. Both cubs were very calm and quiet and did not struggle at all to get away from us, nor did Maddie give the impression of being stressed. Maybe she remembered me after all. I cuddled her, stroked her head and ears and put my nose in her soft fur; she smelled just like a new puppy, not foxy at all. After all, at eight weeks old she was only a baby, and she was adorable.

We were all talking about the things that had happened

in the first couple of weeks and the events that had led to this meeting. After a while I thought we should introduce the cubs to each other. I still remember Angie's worried voice as I edged Maddie ever closer to the new cub. 'Don't let her bite him, be careful, she is a wild fox,' she said. Inch by inch I moved Maddie closer to her new friend until, at last, the cubs were nose to nose. They both seemed quite uninterested at first and kept looking around at all the strange people present. Then Maddie spotted him, she stretched her neck and sniffed at his face a few times. We held our breath as we wondered what her reaction would be. She was wild and he was tame and three weeks younger, but after a bit of sniffing and pretending she had not seen him, she just licked his nose and his face. It was very cute and we took many photographs. We stopped worrying about them fighting and started chatting and thinking of what the new cub would be called.

Foxes are often wrongly perceived as vicious predators and I suggested 'Sid', after Sid Vicious from the punk band, which made us all laugh. Clearly 'Sid' was not vicious at all, and neither was Maddie; the cubs were passed around from one to the other. I could see that Maddie's back legs were not moving and that one of them was held very straight. 'Sid', who was three weeks younger than Maddie was perfect all over. Mind you, Christian thought he was an 'ugly snub-nosed little cub'; little did he know what a beautiful and elegant fox Sid would become in the following months.

Maddie was always very beautiful, and right from day one she held a special place in my heart.

After a while the little foxes tired of all the attention and cuddles. They had a drink and a bit of chicken, and were put back in their separate cages for a rest. They fell asleep almost immediately. We all went outside to inspect the new enclosure. Christian had been working very hard and it was coming on nicely – in fact it was not far off being finished. The enclosure would eventually have lots of big logs in it for the foxes to climb on, as well as a children's slide and a Wendy house. It was going to be a wonderful play area for them.

Scarlett and Darla were outside together in the smaller enclosure at the back of the house. They were a bit wary of all the strangers and kept hiding behind and in the kennel. I gave them each a 'Smart bone' - they resemble rawhide bones but are made with peanut butter instead of hide. Like dogs, foxes like peanut butter, and they seemed to like those nutty bones. Scarlett immediately buried hers behind her kennel and then tried to steal Darla's, which backfired, as I saw Darla with both the bones in her mouth a bit later.

I had one big bone left which I gave to Oscar the dog once we were back inside the house again. That was really comical, because he did nothing with it: he sat looking around with it in his mouth for a good twenty minutes, even tried to get on my lap, then suddenly, in about five seconds flat it was gone. I never even saw him chew it.

I asked if the babies would sleep together in one cage at night but no, they would not, not straightaway; Angie did not want to leave them together in one cage without supervision in the night. The two big cages could be linked together however, so they could see each other and touch noses but not bite. They would have cat carriers in the cages that they could hide in, and would be given some food to eat overnight.

It was with great inner reluctance that I went home with Angie's friends at about five pm; they had left their dog and had to get back for him. I could have stayed all day, and even though I knew Maddie was in good hands I felt as if I was abandoning her all over again. Before I left I took some photos of her in her bed, with her fleece around her – she looked angelic. It had been a delightful afternoon. I left a cooked chicken with Angie to give to the little foxes, and gave some chocolates to Christian. I reckoned he would need the energy to finish that enclosure.

It was quite late when I finally arrived back home. I had taken many photographs and could not wait to put them on my Facebook page so I could share her news and tell people how well she was and how she now had a little companion. There was a great interest in Maddie and within a short time people were following her progress on Facebook. Most people were pleased that she was safe, but there were still a few fanatics who just kept saying that she should be back in the wild or put down. They would not have given her a chance. Exactly how long did they think she would have lasted out there with paralysed back legs, not being able to fend for herself and therefore ultimately dying a miserable death? Oh, I know - they would have put her down 'to prevent further suffering' – where have I heard that expression before? I thought she deserved a chance. Besides, Angie thought she had seen Maddie curl her toes and move her legs.

CHAPTER 8

Sid gets a new name

At first the new black baby, now called 'Angel', cried at night the same way Maddie had that first night with me - after all, he was only five weeks old. I didn't know then that tame-bred cubs were taken from their mother that early. Apparently, in America, they take them from their mothers as early as two to three weeks sometimes; mind you, the rules seem to change all the time and some breeders now leave the cubs with Mum until they are six to eight weeks old when they are fully weaned. During the day, when there was supervision, Maddie and Angel were together in one cage, but at night they were still separate, although they could see each other and touch noses.

It did not take long for Maddie to start taking a very healthy interest in her new friend; he certainly was an incentive for her to start moving, as Angie had hoped. She dragged herself over to his corner when he was asleep, and would start to bite his tail and pull his ears in order to wake him up and encourage him to play. Sometimes she pinned him down in a corner of the cage, and more than once he squealed when she was a little too rough. Maddie even tried sitting up every now and then – not always successfully, mind you - but I saw photos of her sitting up for the first time. Her new friend really motivated her to move, because like all cubs she just wanted to play. She regularly crawled to the other side of the crate where Angel was sleeping, dragging her legs, sometimes making it onto three legs and sometimes falling over.

Then, exactly four weeks after I found her, there was some bad news from Angie. Her husband was worried about Maddie's tail. About a quarter of the way up from the end a little lump had appeared, and he thought that part of her tail was dying and that she might lose it; he had prepared Angie for the fact that it might just drop off. We were both hoping he would be wrong, as it would mean Maddie would lose the white tip to her tail which is such a distinctive feature of most foxes. I also wondered, yet again, if she had been run over after all or had just caught her tail – so many questions remained unanswered.

A few days later came the news I had been dreading: the end part of Maddie's tail had died and fallen off, although the wound was dry and she was not in any pain.

Now she was not only disabled but also disfigured, poor little baby. I felt upset and could not imagine what she would look like now.

It is possible that Angel had hurt Maddie's tail whilst playing, because it became red and infected and she had to have antibiotics. Obviously he did not know that she had bad legs and occasionally he was a bit rough - as little boys can be. Maddie still had a bath every day, during which she had hydrotherapy with Christian massaging her legs, and now, once she was dried, wound powder was applied to keep her tail stump dry.

Four weeks after they first met, Angie was certain that Maddie could defend herself by kicking her new friend away when she had enough of him, so Maddie and Angel were allowed to be together all the time and he stopped crying at night. The babies were sleeping together in the same cage - so sweet. Angie also told me that Maddie was a bully, always waking Angel up, pulling his ears, his tail, pinning him down in a corner and play-fighting with him. Naughty girl.

I asked where the name 'Angel' had come from and Angie explained that it was from the *Angel* TV series about vampires. I was not familiar with this and had to Google it to learn who they were. It used to be a popular series in the USA, and it was Angie's American friend, Heather, who had suggested the name. The name 'Darla' had come from the same series.

The interest in the new cubs, especially Maddie, remained high and the questions most frequently and regularly asked were 'how are her legs now?', 'when will she be released to the wild?' and 'is she walking yet?' I found these frequent same questions very frustrating, because it was such early days. It also made Angie very sad. She and Christian were doing all they could and there was definite progress as Maddie was beginning to move her legs. However, the vet reckoned it would take time, maybe even a very long time - months rather than weeks. Angie told me how anxious she felt every morning when she entered Maddie's room, wondering if her patient would still be alive. Like human babies, there is a chance of fits or sudden death in baby foxes during their first year, not unlike a cot death. Can you imagine it? What a worrying thought.

Some days, Angel and Maddie played in the massive bathroom. In a past life this room had been a downstairs bedroom, so it really was a huge room with lino on the floor. The advantage of playing in there was that the lino was smoother than the carpet in the lounge; chasing Angel on the carpet rubbed and made Maddie's backside and legs sore. The cubs played with their toys and explored happily in that bathroom. In the morning they always were given an egg each; Angel frequently stole Maddie's egg, walking around with two eggs in his mouth and trying to hide them. She chased him to within an inch of his life and would not let him get away with it. It was incredible how fast she could move. She was also a bit fatter now than Angel, but he was getting bigger and fast.

This is where I found Maddie in the gutter

Shocked and traumatised, but no visible injuries

A very suspicious look from a smelly and dirty cub the next morning

Gloves on, those little teeth are sharp!

We're off to the vet

I thought it was a boy and
named her Eddie

Safe in the arms of her new carer

She looked
exquisite.....

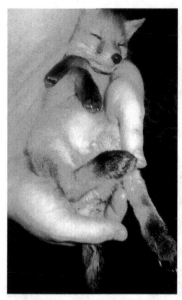

That's not a boy

Maddie in the bath (photo by Angie)

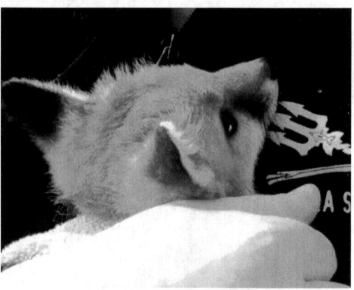

Loving my new daddy, he's a Sea Shepherd (photo by Angie)

Being dried with a fluffy towel
(photo byAngie)

Can you feed me please?
(photo by Angie)

Christian feeds Maddie breakfast
(photo by Angie)

Come on, you can do it!
(photo by Angie)

A lovely new friend for me, yay! (photo by Maggie Bruce)

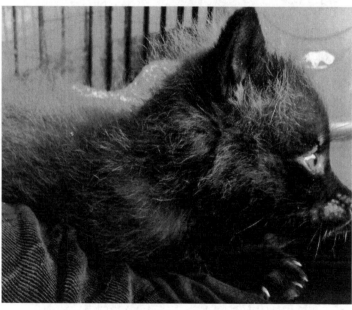

Angel, the 'ugly, snubnosed little cub' (photo by Maggie Bruce)

First meeting with Angel (photo by Maggie Bruce)

One in each hand (photo by Angie)

So very beautiful, so innocent at about eight weeks old

Mmmmm, chicken!

Thirsty now

Safe with Christian

Hold on - whose crate is this anyway?
(photo by Angie)

Maddie and Angel sleeping together (photo by Angie)

Angel at five weeks - he's still got blue eyes (photo by Maggie)

I'll lick the cream off your cake, yum!

Visitors are so tiring

Sleeping Maddie (photo by Maggie)

Happy Maddie, outside on her wheels
for the first time (photo by Angie)

What do I do now? (photo by Angie)

Scarlett smells the roses (photo by Angie)

I'm worn out...YAWN

OMG, is that a girl fox?

Evie wants to play, Angel.....

I'm hiding under here....

Wheeeee, down the slide!

A cuddle with Angel in July (photo by Christian)

Have the visitors gone?

Shall we go for a walk, Maddie? (photo by Christian)

I hate those big red gloves

I want to go the other way

Enough now, take me home

Look, there are ponies in that field!

And there is Rosie, the stray cat

She loved Angie's curtains - hahaha

Tired from wrecking that sofa

Maddie, growing up, September

What a gorgeous girl

No, Angel, that's my steak

Darla and Angel on top of their play house

Darla, that's my champagne!

Angel found Maggie's handbag

I am a princess, this is my castle

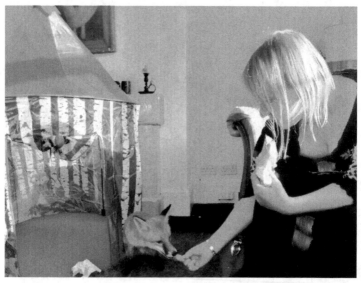

Emma has oat cookies - yum yum!

Oh look, an unattended handbag and a pair of boots - ha!

I think I can hear Santa coming down the chimney

No one is looking, I'll open this Christmas present

That is not how you wear the Santa hat, Maddie

Put Angel down, Chris, I want to play with him

I've got chicken - SIT! (photo by Maggie Bruce)

Mmm, I love scented candles

'What big red bauble, where?'

Having fun on Christmas day 2014
(photo by Angie)

Is it safe to come out?

I just want to be an Andrex puppy

Playing hide and seek (photo by Maggie)

Angel with Anneka Svenska, doing their bit for the anti-fur campaign (photo used with permission)

Mac, the Macaw

Oscar says goodbye

March 2015 - Happy
1st Birthday Maddie

Lewie, Maddie's love
interest (photo by Angie)

Scarlett and Oscar as babies
(photo by Angie)

Scarlett, hiding in her house
(photo by Angie)

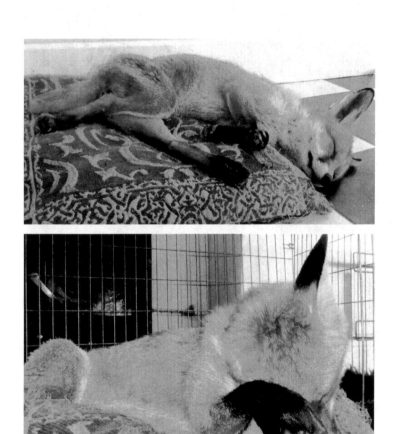

Maddie, the sleeping beauty

Maddie's new friend Byron, eight weeks old (photo: Angie)

Maddie and Byron resting together (photo: Angie)

July 2015: Maddie has got over her teenage tantrums; she is a beautiful gentle vixen again who loves to be made a fuss of.

CHAPTER 9

Birthday celebrations

The next time I saw Maddie was four weeks after the first foxy convention. It was on June 10th, a couple of weeks before my birthday in fact. It would also be our friend Maggie's birthday a few days before mine, so a double celebration. We were going to have an early birthday party, and with five other fox lovers invited, plus Angie and Christian, we were eight in number all together. It was the 'second foxy convention', as we called it.

We were in the big lounge overlooking the garden, and when I entered the room I saw no baby foxes at all. There were some blue balloons on the floor, and I assumed the foxes had been playing with them, but their cage was empty, so where were they? 'Playing hide and seek' was the answer and, on cue, Angel suddenly appeared from behind one of the chairs. I could not believe my eyes - how he had grown in the four weeks since I had last seen him! His legs seemed really long, his snub nose had elongated, and he was over twice the size he had been four weeks earlier. He was running about the room, darting around the furniture, under the sofas and behind the curtains. The fireplace had been blocked with a picture and there was a guard around it. Can you imagine a fox climbing up the chimney? Try explaining that to the fire brigade.

Maddie also looked much bigger and was beginning to look like a proper fox; her fur was a slightly darker red than previously. She scooted across the room after Angel, mainly pulling herself along with her front legs whilst pushing with one of her back legs; it looked a bit like a sideways bunny hop, but she was remarkably fast. Just before we arrived she had even climbed to the top of her cage and got her right back leg stuck, possibly spraining it. I could see how her back legs were sticking out at a peculiar angle. I also noticed the wound on her tail - poor baby.

It must have been a bit stressful for the little foxes to see so many people, as they were only used to two people and now there were six strangers as well. Maddie and Angel continued hiding behind the sofa, with Angel chewing at the paint on the skirting board and Maddie watching - and learning, no doubt. It needed Christian and me to get her out from underneath the sofa, she was so quick. I grabbed Angel by the scruff of his neck whilst he was not looking.

He gave a little squeal of protest, but now we could have a cuddle.

Once Christian had caught Maddie she was wrapped in a piece of vet bed and I could snuggle her. I was very careful not to hurt her. Once again she sat still on my lap and allowed me to stroke her ears and bury my face in the fur on top of her head – she still smelled like a puppy, and I kissed her gently on her head. These were also questions I frequently had to answer about Maddie on Facebook: 'What does she smell like? Can you cuddle her?'

Two of the other guests, avid fox lovers, had not met any fox cubs previously and were quite overwhelmed when they were given the babies to hold. Angel was fine once he had been caught and was quite happy to be passed around and cuddled; when he grew tired he just fell asleep on someone's lap. With his tongue sticking out, he looked very cute. Everyone was taking photos of these exquisite cubs.

After a while Maddie was getting slightly stressed by all the attention and started breathing quite fast with her mouth open. Angie thought that she might be feeling hot and suggested that Christian give her a drink and a little bit of chopped chicken. She licked up some of the milk and had a few bites of chicken; then Christian sat down on the other side of the room with Maddie to reassure her and calm her down. Awake again now, Angel came along and polished off the rest of her food and her milk.

Once more we had lunch and cream cakes and bottle of champagne - it was a celebration, after all. I had a little cream and jam doughnut and crawled slowly across the floor to where Christian was sitting with Maddie. Clearly he had managed to calm her down and she felt safe with her human daddy. I dipped my finger in the cream and jam and held it out to Maddie. She was either going to bite me, ignore me or eat it. Sure enough, her sweet tooth emerged and she started licking my finger clean; it was the sweetest experience ever. She did not bite at all. Her tongue was really soft and smooth, not rough like a cat's. It surprised me, and I did it a couple of times more till all the cream and jam had gone, joking about how I was now going to take that doughnut back to M&S to complain there had been no filling in it - but regardless of Maddie licking all the cream and jam off it, I ate it instead.

It was getting quite warm in the room and the air conditioning unit was put on. You cannot have windows or doors open when you have foxes in a room; they can climb really well and would be gone before you knew what had happened. Maybe not Maddie with her wonky legs, but Angel would.

At that moment Angie came back into the room carrying a big birthday cake with candles alight – such a surprise. Before I could say anything the candles were immediately extinguished by the air-conditioning, which was blowing cool air from above at quite a fast rate. It was very funny, and we burst out laughing. I was so touched to think Angie had gone through the trouble of getting a cake and immediately welled up. Oh dear – not again! The older I get, the more emotional I get and I am always extremely moved by unexpected kindness from other people. Dear oh dear. We moved the cake to the coffee table, lit the candles again and sang 'Happy Birthday' for Maggie and me. Then the two of us blew out the candles and cut the cake together.

With both cubs now asleep in the cage, we all went outside to inspect the new enclosure, which was finished. It looked beautiful. The logs and bark chips gave it a very natural look and the green artificial floor, which could easily be hosed down, made it all look really wonderful. It was huge and there was a Wendy house in it and a slide, as well as plenty of space for a table and some chairs in the corner so we could sit down and watch the foxes play and clamber over the logs whilst drinking our tea.

Darla was in her room, but the sliding door was open and she soon came out to see what was going on. She was very inquisitive and friendly, examining cameras and pulling shoes. However, because Darla and Scarlett had been fighting recently they had been separated from each other. We had to go through the connecting gate to see Scarlett, who was in her own enclosure, but she hid in her kennel as soon as she saw us. She is not keen on strangers and we only caught a few glimpses of her. Angie says 'she's only got to hear people talking in the field next door and she hides for a week!'

Angie thought Darla might have come into her first season in February, so probably her hormones were still playing up, who knows? They never had Darla when she was a baby, so they did not know what she had been like growing up. She was not aggressive at all towards any of us and we could touch her, albeit sporadically, as she just ran away when we reached out to her. She looked magnificent with her silver eyebrows and flanks, and huge compared to the cubs. We sat outside chatting and taking photographs for quite a while before we had to go home.

Angie mentioned that she had ordered some wheels for Maddie now that she was a bit bigger, so that she would be able to go out. They had to come all the way from America and she was hoping they would arrive soon. That way Maddie's bottom and back legs would be supported off the ground, which was important because not only would it encourage her to use her legs and build up her muscles, it would also stop her getting carpet burns from chasing after Angel when they played in the living room.

It was lovely to think that the little foxes would now be able to go outside, but obviously they could not just go out with Darla straight away as they did not know how she would react, therefore a few experiments were carried out. Angel is a silver fox like Darla, so he was first to go in the enclosure to meet Darla. Christian called him the 'test dummy'. He was taken outside and left inside his cage in Darla's enclosure. How would she react? Would she be aggressive towards him or accept him? Aww, it was so sweet! She retrieved some of her own cached food and pushed it towards him through the bars - what a loveable, caring girl. I wondered if she thought he was her cub. Foxes usually make wonderful mothers.

Over the next few days Angie and Christian became convinced that Darla would not attack Angel and he was left to play outside with her. Look at the video (http://youtu.be/t9hWWdkyzEE) and you will see that he already had the agile grace of an adult fox with very long legs, and you can see how he could look after himself.

A few days later Maddie was also introduced to Darla, who accepted her too, giving her own food to Maddie. You may wonder why Maddie was not with Scarlett, but Darla and Scarlett had another big fight; we thought it possible that Scarlett was jealous, and maybe Darla was trying to protect *her* cubs when Scarlett came near. Who knows? It was Darla who had accepted the little cubs and the result was that the older foxes had to be separated.

It was such an exciting time for Maddie. She loved playing outside with Angel and Darla, who just treated them like her cubs, it was delightful to see. Angie sent me a video clip of the three of them playing outside. Although Maddie was clearly having a great time, I could not help but feel a bit sad at the sight of her half tail and her dragging legs as she was scooting about – I knew she could stand and kick, she just wasn't doing it, and although she was fatter

than Angel she was still so small in comparison. See
http://youtu.be/_DwahjkIXBE

CHAPTER 10

Where is my daddy?

During July a few unexpected events occurred that affected Maddie badly. Christian had taken up some new studies and had to go away on a course for a few days; Maddie was left in Angie's care. This change in routine did not go down well with Miss Maddie - how dare he leave her! She hissed and growled at Angie when she bathed Maddie, and the little red patient generally behaved like a diva, even trying to nip Angie.

Her waking hours were spent playing with Darla and Angel in the enclosure, which she loved, but which made her bottom very sore. She had to have nappy cream applied to help heal her and she had to rest in her cage with a collar on until her bottom was better. She needed her wheels to get her up off the floor; hopefully they would arrive soon.

Angie and Christian decided that her playtime with

Angel had to be limited in order for her backside to heal properly. They would now just have an hour of romping together each day and then Maddie would rest in the big cage - that way she would know he was still around. She also needed a couple of steroid injections for an infection in her tail wound.

Maddie was not impressed with her shortened playtime with Angel, and Angie had to start wearing gloves when she had to deal with Maddie. She decided to put Maddie's cage into the new conservatory which served as a breakfast room and was off the kitchen. There she could be with Angie and could look out of the windows at the dogs in the garden; she also had the company of Mac, the macaw. The floors in the kitchen and breakfast room have smooth ceramic tiles, so they would not chafe her bottom and leg when she played there with her toys. She loved to play with her toys, but there were also other new and interesting activities that a fox cub could indulge in, such as pulling all the dirty bedding out of the rubbish bag, shredding heaps of newspapers, playing fetch the ball, throwing dog biscuits around, catching flies at the windows and moving the freezer around, which was on sliders. Her favourite game was climbing up and swinging off the curtains, using her teeth and front claws to hold on. She was so funny to watch.

The wheels duly arrived from America and Christian came back from his course, which was good, as it needed two people to get the harness and wheels on Maddie. Well, you didn't think she was going to stand there and step into the harness, did you? The wheels were pink, as befits a girlie fox, and I was looking forward to seeing Maddie mobilising with this aid. I have already mentioned that foxes will get neophobic when they get older. They just do not like changes in their environment or new routines. I have seen wild urban foxes act very suspiciously and scared in the garden of my friend Maggie when she left a bowl of yoghurt on the lawn for them for the first time, you would have thought that any minute it was going to jump up and attack them from the way they acted.

Chaos ensued: when the harness had to be slipped on over her head, a new and therefore terrifying experience for a fox cub, Angie and Christian had a major struggle. Maddie went berserk; she bit Christian so badly that he had to resort to wearing thick, long red gauntlets. She behaved like a monster and it earned her the nickname 'Miss Bite'. Once she was strapped in she was fine. Would you believe it?

Under supervision and with a short lead attached, Maddie was now let out into the enclosure with Darla and Angel, which she loved. Angel took the lead into his mouth sometimes, as if he was taking her for a walk, but clearly Maddie did not have a clue how to cope with this new way of mobilising: she could not go around corners, could not reverse, got stuck between the logs and tipped herself over onto her back or her side. Oh dear, she definitely needed L-plates; but the first time I saw a photo of Maddie standing outside in her wheels she looked so happy that I had tears running down my face. Vroom, vroom, surely my girl would get the hang of it soon, or so I thought. Angie and Christian had expected Maddie to have to get used to the wheels, but in her eagerness to get going, she took off into the garden like a rocket, and as a result a long lead had to be attached to maintain some measure of control. Furthermore, whilst she first just let her legs drag, she occasionally started to take some steps when they were walking her in the garden. It was a promising start.

Then another calamity in Maddie's young life: Christian had to go away again. He was only gone for a few days, but this time, when he came home, Maddie wanted nothing to do with him. She hissed at him, tried to bite him, ran off, and went to sit at Angie's feet. She clearly did not love her daddy any longer. It did not go down well with Christian, but he was now the big baddie in Maddie's life: she had transferred her affections to Angie, following her around in the kitchen like a small red puppy and watching her all the time as she washed vet beds and cleaned bowls, prepared meals and saw to the dogs. A baby gate between the kitchen and the breakfast room stopped her getting into too much trouble and kept her safe from the dogs. As far as Maddie was concerned her daddy had deserted her, so she did not trust him any longer. He was mortified. Undoubtedly the hostility towards Christian was caused by him being away; Maddie must have thought he had abandoned her and it was as if she had turned her back on him. However, the enmity continued, as did the battle with the harness and the wheels. If only Maddie could have understood that the harness and wheels would help her rehabilitation.

Angie contemplated buying a new harness, one that would fit across her chest and not go over her head. Maybe that would get Maddie into the wheels without the major temper tantrums and the biting. Dream on! Miss Bite was just as bad and she only had to catch sight of Christian and his big red gloves and she would start to growl and hide.

What else could be done? They tried supporting her back legs with just a small cat harness around her back end, using it as a sling. Initially we thought this might be less traumatic than the harness and wheels as a means of taking her for a walk in the garden. Indeed, a couple of weeks later she stood up in the correct position for over a minute, looking through the patio doors – she was watching Rosie, the stray cat, in the garden. It was such exciting news and it meant yet another step in the right direction.

However, when he saw her, the vet said that with the cat harness around her back, her spine was in the wrong position, so it would be better to use the wheels. Because she put up such a fight it took a long time to put her harness on, and we discussed whether we would perhaps be able to adjust the harness with Velcro straps so it would not have to go over her head - maybe that would stop 'Miss Alligator' from snapping.

All this trouble, yet Maddie *was* making progress; one of her legs was starting to move a little when walking and she was now sitting on top of her legs instead of having them stuck out in front of her. She was eating well and growing. If only she had been calmer and had not been biting so much, they would have been able to treat her a great deal easier. Yet you could not blame her, Maddie was feisty and did not understand that we were trying to help her. She did not know she was disabled, and we were not going to tell her. She didn't know any better and seemed happy enough spending her days playing, eating, sleeping and getting up to mischief. On the other hand it was so important for her to get up, as we did not want her to get sore on her bottom or on the leg she sat on. We just had to wait and be patient.

One night in the middle of July, Angie was awoken by a terrible shrieking from Scarlett's enclosure: a rat had got in from the garden through the bars and Scarlett could not get to it. The next night Darla and Angel were put in that kennel together, they caught it and that was the end of the rat. Like me, Angie always felt sorry for anything that died. 'It couldn't help being a rat', she said, but you can't have rats coming in. Yes, July was an eventful month and also, because they were now going outside, Maddie and Angel were vaccinated that week and all seemed well once more.

I made arrangements to come and see Angie again at the end of July, and had booked myself into the Travelodge for a couple of nights. Yes, *that* Travelodge, the one I had not been able to find the first time I drove back from her house three months earlier. As soon as I arrived I spotted a beautiful tortoiseshell cat in the garden sitting by the pond, and I wondered if it was another of Angie's charges, but no, apparently this was Rosie, the stray cat.

Other people would also be at the house for the afternoon, including another of our friends with her family *and* her pet silver fox, Evie, who was the same age as Angel; we thought they might like to play together. I had brought a small trampoline to go in the enclosure for the foxes to play on, sleep on, hide under or just destroy.

Maddie was in a very bad mood that day. She had cystitis - the vet had warned us this might happen and so she was left to rest in her room and had been given a steroid injection. She had been bathed that morning and she was stressed enough as it was without all the visiting strangers, including a strange fox. When I went to see Maddie in her room, there was an aloofness about her that had not been there previously. I tried to feed her a little yoghurt through the bars. She took a few licks but was not very enthusiastic and tried to hide under her vet bed. I felt quite sorry for her. I was also acutely aware that in the future, there would probably be no further cuddles with my little rescued baby.

After lunch, Darla was locked up elsewhere, as Angie did not trust her with a strange fox, and we spent the afternoon outside in the large enclosure with Angel and

Evie, the two silver babies. It was the funniest scenario ever. We were so surprised when, having expected the two young foxes to play together like puppies, our beautiful boy, Angel, appeared to be scared of girlie fox, Evie, who looked very pretty in her pink harness. Instead of playing with her, he hid behind the wendy house, behind the chairs, under the slide or he sat on someone's lap squealing and whimpering like a baby. He wanted nothing to do with her. It was incredible, we could not believe it and called him a wuss. It must have been such a disappointment for Evie's owners, who had made a very long journey to get there. Evie herself was quite interested in her potential playmate, but he wasn't having any of it and would not play. I have since learnt that whereas puppies are quite happy to play together, strange foxes are not. They are more like cats in their behaviour, and are very territorial, even as cubs.

After all the visitors had departed Angie, Christian and I brought Maddie back into the lounge and I suggested taking her for a walk in the garden, as she had been indoors all day. Christian was tired and did not seem all that keen, or up for a fight with Maddie, if the truth be known, but with the big red gloves on he and Angie got her in the wheels so I could take her for a walk. As she had grown a bit, the wheel frame had to be adjusted so that it was the proper height and length for her.

With the long lead attached to her harness, Christian and I went into the garden. Once more Maddie set off like a rocket, refusing to use her back legs. How disappointing. At this rate they would never be strong enough to stand on, let alone walk on. However, after a short distance she put her feet down. She also tried to wriggle away from us by pulling her head back through the harness, finally coming unstuck and ending up like a turtle on its back with her feet in the air. I decided that the Velcro straps possibly needed tightening a little, so I bent forward to do that. Huge mistake! She snapped her head round and bit my left hand in a sort of 'get off me' movement, then quick as a flash she whipped her face round and bit my right hand.

I was now bleeding from both hands and Christian looked worried, but I grabbed the little snapper firmly in the scruff of her neck with my right hand and clamped my left hand over her snout.

'Quick, Christian, put those straps back on tight!' I said. For a tiny fox cub she was very strong and I could only just keep a hold of her long enough for him to adjust her harness and get her in it properly again. Naughty girl! - I was only trying to help her. All I could do was to lick my wounds and thank goodness my tetanus shots were up to date.

It soon stopped hurting and then we were off again around the garden, Maddie at a running pace with us following behind, holding on to the lead and trying not to get the wheels stuck in the rose bushes, trying to stop her running straight into the pond or to stop her eating something she should not. It was not easy, I can tell you that, and I realised Christian and Angie must have had their hands full on a daily basis with the little monster. I found that out when I tried to hold the lead myself to walk her around the garden. Foxes never seem to just walk, they always seem to run, and even the ones I watch at home in my garden always seem to be in a hurry. A couple more times we had to rescue Maddie again from getting herself entangled in her lead and from carrying out her 'turned-up turtle' impersonation. I let Christian do it this time as he was the one wearing the gloves.

At times, Maddie now seemed to hold one of her back legs across her tummy, which was odd as she had not done that previously. We wondered if she had sprained it or had got it stuck in the cage wires again as we had all seen her climb up on the inside the cage on another day. Christian blamed himself and thought that it was caused by something he had done wrong, maybe with the other cat harness, but I had seen her climb two feet up inside her cage that afternoon and had also seen her get one of her back legs stuck on another occasion, so it could not be something he had done. She had probably sprained a tendon or wrenched her hip.

Consequently, Maddie was booked in for an X-ray of her spine and back legs after the weekend, which meant a general anaesthetic at the vet's surgery. This would be a risky business, especially for such a tiny fox - not to mention for the vet, as Maddie hated him with a passion. She was nearly four and a half months old now, but still really small.

With me wounded and Christian exhausted we called it

a day with the outdoor exercise, left Maddie to rest, and ordered a fine Chinese take-away which we ate outside on the patio accompanied by stray cat Rosie, purring on my lap, and bare-chested Mac the macaw on his perch shouting 'hello' every now and then. Prior to Angie getting him eighteen years ago, he had been kept in a small cage for thirteen years. He was never let out and became so stressed that he had pulled all his chest feathers out. As a result they would not grow again and if, occasionally, a small red feather did appear on his chest he pulled that out too. He was a very large bird with lovely red and white markings on his face and a magnificent tail. We all sat outside till late and I left the family around ten-thirty pm to check into my room at the Travelodge for the night.

Chapter 11

I get a new cat

The next day, Sunday, Angie and Christian were out, so I did not see Maddie till Monday, when I visited to see everyone again… and to pick up Rosie the stray cat to take her home with me. She seemed to have adopted me over the weekend, sitting on my lap and purring.

There had been no objections from her potential new owner to me giving her a permanent safe home. In fact it was Angie who had suggested it, as she was worried about Rosie moving to her new home, which was on a main road. Rosie had lived outside in Angie's garden for a week or so by then and someone was going to take her in after he had moved house, especially as she had lived with him previously.

Rosie had a bit of a chequered history. She had lived in

about five different homes already, including a spell or two in kennels whilst various owners were moving house, splitting up, developing allergies, 'pets forbidden' by landlords and so forth. It was thought she was healthy and was about eight years old. She was vaccinated and micro-chipped. Angie did know that Rosie's mother had been rescued years ago from floating out to sea by clinging on to a tyre. Rosie's mother had been taken to the vet's surgery and had given birth soon afterwards to five kittens, one of them Rosie, a very pretty tortoiseshell girl who went to a friend of Angie's daughter. As I had lost one of my twin tabbies to diabetes the previous year, there was a vacancy in my house and I thought Rosie would appreciate the quiet and stable environment of my house and garden.

She was a beautiful cat and seemed very affectionate. In order not to upset her tummy, I was given a bag of dry cat food to take home with me, the same food that she had been sharing outside with Angie's cats, and I hoped I would be home in time to buy a second litter tray, as she would have to be kept in for a while.

Maddie had been very happy playing with Angel that morning and the two cubs had been chasing each other and rolling about all the time, it was so sweet to see. After running around the room with Angel and being videoed, Maddie was asleep in her cage when I left, and I blew her a kiss.

The journey home was extremely eventful, to say the

very least. Not fifteen miles into the trip, after a spluttering noise, a terrible stench pervaded the car. Oh NO, Rosie had suffered an attack of explosive diarrhoea, and it was dripping through the bars and onto the seat belt that strapped the carrier onto the passenger seat. I was horrified - what was I going to do? With a new cat in the car it was obviously not an option to open the windows or doors, as she might have run off.

Fortunately there was a carrier bag in the car with my newspaper in it and a packet of wet wipes. I looked for somewhere to park, stopped and carefully opened the door of the cat basket. Rosie thought this was very sociable; she walked right through the stinking mess, sat on my lap, and started to purr. I tried not to breathe through my nose but felt quite queasy. The smell was foul and I did not know where to start. I decided to clean the basket first. Gingerly, I took the filthy paper and fleece out of the cat basket and put them in the plastic bag, trying not to get any mess on my fingers or to disturb Rosie too much, as I did not want her to start walking around in the car, covered in dirt as she was. I then cleaned the inside of the basket with wet wipes, working around Rosie, who quite happily remained sitting on my lap, purring. But I was quite concerned...this was supposed to be a cat that had never been sick; perhaps it was the stress of being in the car.

I put my clean newspaper in the basket and then set about cleaning Rosie's legs and paws, backside and tail, during which process she was quite docile, before putting her back in the basket. Phew, at last I was able to open the windows. However, she had left an awful mess on my lap and on the passenger seat; there was no way I could drive another 120 miles or so in that state. I carried on cleaning my trousers, the seat and the outside of the cage as best I could, and blessed my lucky stars that I had been in possession of a full packet of one hundred wet wipes. Last but not least, I cleaned my hands and put all the dirty wipes in the plastic bag.

Fortunately, the rest of the journey was quite uneventful, Rosie just went to sleep and, naturally, due to all the upheaval, I missed the turn for that A1 again and had to make a detour to find it. It was a good thing that I had the map with me this time. With the car windows now open and a delay of nearly an hour I carried on. I stopped at a big service station and ditched the plastic bag with its rank contents and went to wash my hands properly. My trousers had dried, but they were still quite malodorous, so I used the soap from the washroom to have another clean-up session.

Time was getting on and I realised that I probably would not be home in time to buy another litter tray, so I went into one of the shops and ask for an empty cardboard box. I also bought some plain cooked chicken breasts, as I thought Rosie might be hungry by now. A bit of plain cooked chicken should not upset her tummy. I tore off little pieces and fed them to her; she was very hungry indeed. I thought she was thin, as I could feel her bones when I stroked her and felt sorry for her, she was such a sweet cat. However, I now became worried about my other cat, Molly; I wanted to get back as soon as possible. I wondered what her reaction would be to the new addition. Not only had I been away for three days, I was also bringing home a new 'sister'. It probably would not be well received... cats are so territorial.

Once back at home I left Rosie in the car whilst sorting out two separate litter trays. There followed a major re-organisation at home: I decided that Rosie would stay downstairs for now with the cat flap locked and Molly would be upstairs, as she always sleeps on my bed anyway and I did not want to disturb her routine too much. Molly's litter tray would be on the mat in the hall downstairs and Rosie's would be on some newspaper in the living room, that way they could be kept apart. I cut the sides of the cardboard box down and lined the bottom of the box with the cut-off pieces and a layer of litter. I also wanted to know if her diarrhoea had been a one-off or if she was in fact sick.

My word, what had I taken on? To cut a long story short, I spent all of August and most of September keeping cats, food and litter trays apart, disinfecting and cleaning, making weekly visits with Rosie to the vet, cleaning up diarrhoea three to five times per day, administering cleaning fluid for her ears, eye drops and flea and worm treatment. Following my vet's advice I cooked plain rice, fish and chicken – Rosie only ate the chicken and left the fish and rice every time. I had to order different veterinary food for her; she was underweight and her fur looked dull.

When she passed some blood one night, I panicked and took her for an emergency appointment. You know cats never have an emergency during vet's surgery opening hours, don't you? She was given a week's course of antibiotic tablets for her intestines as the duty vet thought she might have colitis. Oh joy, tablets for a cat!

Rosie drooled, coughed, retched, spat the pills out, bit and scratched me. I despaired; all I had wanted to do was to give her a nice home, and now all these problems. My face was scratched and I had more salicylic acid on me than she had in her ears, as she shook her head vigorously after each application. Nevertheless, her ears got better but I then had to put antibiotic eardrops in her ears as they were inflamed. Still, a slight overall improvement followed, if you can call diarrhoea two or three times a day an improvement.

However, things were not right yet and my vet suggested we should test her poo, so I duly collected three faecal samples, which were sent off; all came back negative for various nasty infections and infestations such as salmonella, giardia, trichomonas, campylobacter and parasites. Having excluded everything else, the vet then wondered if she might have an allergy, so he suggested another two-week course of antibiotics to heal her gut, hypoallergenic food and a six-week course of weekly vitamin B12 injections. He was convinced he could cure her. Oh no, not a two-week course of antibiotic pills again? I asked if he would like to move in for a couple of weeks which he politely refused. However, instead of pills he gave me antibiotic suspension, which I could just squirt into Rosie's mouth with a syringe twice a day - this proved much easier than the pills of course.

Slowly Rosie improved and put on some weight. I combed her fur every day and it became all shiny. I gave her nothing but her special food and water, and with the antibiotics and the course of B12 injections her diarrhoea finally stopped; it had taken nearly eight weeks and I had spent about £800 on my new cat, not counting her new bed, toys and a new large litter tray. She always used her litter tray, and after seven weeks I had finally let her go outside, given her the run of the house and let her mix with Molly, who took an instant dislike to her and hissed at her every time she had to pass her. I bought some Feliway to soothe them, but nine months later on they still are not the best of friends. Rosie can be quite playful and her running around scares the living daylights out of Molly, who has always been a slightly nervous cat.

To make matters worse, at the end of September, Molly's diabetes returned, possibly because of the stress of having a new cat in the house, she had been in remission for seven months. She is thirteen and a half and needs to be injected with insulin twice a day now. I do her regular blood tests myself and email the results to the vet. He is happy for me to treat her, and so far she is well controlled and has not lost any weight.

Talking about age, Rosie's second owner was found through her microchip and after a lot of red tape she is now officially registered to me. It turned out she was twelve years old, not eight. Angie could not have known any of this as Rosie had always been with other people, in kennels or living rough outside. Rosie soon made herself at home, sleeping everywhere except in the nice new bed I had bought her, typical!

It's May now; Molly is still diabetic and Rosie is still suffering from an odd skin lesion around her left eye and has had yet more vet visits, steroids and antibiotics, so we are now about £1200 down all together. Sweet cat though, very affectionate, very beautiful, very expensive. Oh well, can't take it with me, can I? I do wish she would not attack the little ginger tabby next door though, especially as she tolerates every other cat in the garden. She's my ASBO cat and now has a harness and lead to stop her leaving my garden when the little ginger one is outside.

CHAPTER 12

Maddie makes friends with the vet

Back to Maddie now, it is her story after all. Her X-rays at the end of July had shown that she had a birth defect in the bones of her right hind leg; there had never been any breaks in her spine or legs. There were four options: Harry could amputate her leg (shock, horror) operate on that leg to realign the bones (painful and difficult, with no guarantee of success), put her to sleep or wait and see if she would eventually walk, albeit with a wobble. The decision was unanimous – we would wait and see. No way was Angie willing to have her put down or to have her leg amputated, so she told her husband what he could do with his scalpel.

Maddie seemed pleased with that decision, as she

promptly made friends with her vet. In the evenings Harry sat in the conservatory/breakfast kitchen, aka Maddie's and Mac's room; he watched the cricket on TV and Maddie now started to sit right next to him by his feet and started to watch cricket with him. He was her new best friend. It was so funny – she was fascinated and could not take her eyes off the TV, stretching her neck to see the screen better. The TV was even turned around a little so she could watch it from her bed – talk about spoilt. I suggested they might as well give her give her the remote control, so she could chose her own TV programmes, but that idea was rejected and the remote was put well out of reach, unlike the one Scarlett had got hold of when she was a baby.

Maddie did manage to get hold of a box with an old mobile in it; she ripped it to bits and then tried to play with the phone. She then shredded the box that her wheels had been sent in, including the packaging and the manuals. She was becoming very naughty and it was not as though she didn't have any toys - she had many.

Miss Maddie also revealed a redhead's temper during August; she objected to the cleaner, the gardener, the handyman and the plumber, giving them the evil eye when they came in – how dare they come into her space? She only saw the handyman through the conservatory windows, but she still hissed at him. It was a good thing he could see her, because one day she pulled down a ten-pound bag of bird seed that had been on top of the freezer: she was spinning around with it throwing it all around the room and scooting through it – such a good game. She must have stood up to reach that. Angie told her off and put her back in her cage whilst the mess was cleaned up: Maddie started sulking and tried to bite her. When she was let out again she trashed the kitchen with newspaper balls and ripped a hole in the curtains. She grabbed hold of a Furby's ear, with the result that it started to talk, and you should have seen her face - it was priceless! She was not impressed when Angie took it off her and gave her a very dirty look. When Maddie was naughty she would always watch Angie's face to see if she was going to react. It was a great game, because when Angie shouted 'no!' she would first run away, then promptly try to do it again - it seemed to be pure spite.

Miss Maddie might have been a very naughty fox, but she was so funny to watch. Small in size, she was not small in attitude. She knew her name by now, and at night when Angie or Harry said 'bed, Maddie,' she put herself to bed in her crate, so she could be very good if she wanted to. She always had a midnight feast to go to bed with; usually some cheese, a tomato, some chicken and dog biscuits. She buried it all under her cushion and ate it in the night.

The little minx was now into everything: TV controls, curtains, anything she could reach and get hold of in fact. She opened kitchen cupboards and one day she even got into the laundry bag, which happened to be empty, but Angie had to cut the handle off to free her, as Maddie had got herself entangled in it somehow. She took all the CDs out of the rack in the lounge so they had to be moved elsewhere, and after this she invented a new game: swinging off Angie's curtains. She hung off them and really tugged them as hard as she could. This action lifted her completely off the floor and she would not let go - clearly this was great fun. She was so strong. Angie said to me 'I don't think she needs good back legs, just good teeth, a long neck and front legs'.

The table in the breakfast room had to be moved because Maddie started to chew the legs. She also started to climb up on the outside of her cage, all the better to reach things she was not allowed to reach, such as wires. We had often wondered how she managed to reach things high up, until Harry saw her do it. Whenever I asked 'how is Maddie', the answer was invariably: 'on the naughty step'!

Angie found she spent all her time looking after the animals. It was an incessant round of cleaning, feeding, watching, entertaining and exercising the various animals - and we all knew who took up most of the time. Maddie had grown in length and she needed another adjustment to her wheels, so she was in a strop again, growling and biting. As soon as she saw the red gloves she started hissing. Initially, she was quite bad on her wheels, although gradually she improved. She even started to take some steps when she was outside, but she had to be watched all the time as she liked to nibble things that were no good for her such as Yew tree branches, Ivy and other plants.

Angie sent me a video clip of her trying to perform a

foxy pounce: it looked as if she had her good leg on the floor and her front legs had pulled the rest of her into place. She had so much energy and was racing around the room like a kitten having a mad half an hour. She got all excited, and that was when she did it. It was not very high. Angie had been on the phone and had thought it looked as if she was going to leap. She ignored her at first, but then saw her do it. Sometimes foxes don't lift their legs off the ground to do the leap, and to get the arched back they do not even have to get off the ground, but Maddie was up and off. She had put her breakfast egg under her blanket, then started to arch her back and was into a leap, lifting her bottom and pushing with her back legs. She was definitely trying to do the foxy pounce. The movement was there and she got her bottom about four inches off the ground. We were optimistic and thought 'any day now she will just get up and walk'.

Harry explained that in humans the signals from brain to legs go straight down, whilst in a fox the signals from the brain cross over. This was initially difficult to understand, but whenever I was with her I could see for myself how one day her good leg was the right hind leg and the next day it would be the left hind leg - if you know what I mean. When she was in her wheels her good leg started to work and bend whilst her other leg just hung limp, yet the next day, the leg action might be reversed. It was crazy, but still we felt she was making progress, because now, when sitting up, she pushed up on the bad leg and held her good leg straight out in front of her. In Maddie the signals coming from her brain seemed to be confused. Nonetheless we never lost faith in a recovery of sorts; our patient was a fighter if nothing else, and she did different things all the time.

Her best friend, vet Harry, bought her new toys; she liked balls and chased them around the room. He said he had never seen an animal move so fast on its bottom. He had not known how fast she could race around the room and not normal 'foxy fast', no, she was like a bat out of hell and she was really enjoying it. It was the first time he had witnessed it and he could not believe his eyes.

There was an anxious day towards the end of August when Miss Maddie knocked a bottle of bleach down. She was on the table whilst being put in her harness and wheels. She was so quick that Angie did not even see it until Harry shouted at her: Maddie had bitten through the bottle and it had spilled all over his trousers. They immediately put her face in water and gave her lots of milk to drink. Angie checked her all night but there were no problems; thank god, she had not ingested any - she just ruined Harry's trousers. That was the same day she got into absolutely everything; there is no bleach around usually, but Christian had washed the floor and left it on the table. Maddie was only on that table because they had to put her harness on and she had spotted it – trust her.

A baby gate separated Maddie from the dogs, and it could be put anywhere, depending on where madam was.

She seemed to like the dogs; they often lay nose-to-nose either side of the gate. One of them, Freeway, a Lhasa Apso, was fascinated by Maddie and it was mutual, but he used to sleep high up on a chair so she could not bite him because he was frightened of her. He must have known she could not jump up that high. Freeway was born with a cleft lip and palate and had been taken to the vet to be put to sleep. Harry operated on him instead and he came to live with the rest of the rescues at their house.

With Maddie in the breakfast room lived Mac the macaw. She was captivated by him, especially when he shouted 'hello', and they often sat just looking at each other. Mac had a large cage around him so Miss Maddie could not get to his tail when he climbed down from his perch; she now also wanted pomegranate seeds like him. What a funny fox.

Once outside on her wheels, Maddie wanted to chase the cats and resented being kept in check. She always loved to go and see the two ponies, Billy and Blue, in the big field. As a treat she still played with Angel in the back room, but the bossy little madam frequently chased him into his box. We already knew what a wuss he could be, even though he was now much bigger than she was.

Because Maddie was so naughty and moody, we were beginning to wonder if she had started 'the crazies' earlier than anticipated; after all, this phase can begin as early as August or September, which is where we were now. When fox cubs go through this stage, they are evil little devils. People who are in their first year of a owning a pet fox cannot understand what is happening to their lovable little cub. This is when new owners of pet foxes sometimes decide to get rid of them because they just cannot cope; they do not realise this is just a phase and that it will pass. It must be even worse if you have a wild fox cub, although that does not happen very often, as most of the rescued red foxes are successfully released with other cubs as a new family. However, if you are thinking of getting a tame-bred pet fox, my advice would have to be: think twice unless you have done a great deal of research. They may look like dogs, and roll over purring like cats, but now throw a hyperactive two-year-old toddler in the throes of a tantrum into the equation and you're halfway there.

There are many animals in shelters that would make lovely, devoted pets, unlike a fox, which does as it pleases. Pet foxes are very beautiful and come in a variety of colours, but you would have to be totally committed to them; you can't leave them, they need a big outside space and are expensive to keep. They also need a lot of exercise and cannot be off-lead. Somebody asked if they could be litter trained. The answer is no – about one in 20 pet foxes will choose to use a puppy pad or litterbox most of the time, but never always. It is their basic nature to poo and pee on everything that is theirs: their food, their beds, their toys, everything – it is what all foxes do in nature, it is their instinct.

CHAPTER 13

The Maddiegator

September passed in much the same fashion in Maddieland. She had however developed a new movement by now; she would cross her hind legs and hop. This pushed her up when she moved across the floor. Angie said: 'She gets about half-way up as she goes along and this might be what we have been waiting for. The leg that bends under her can push up in that position and then the other leg just slides forward. So there is definitely movement and communication between the two legs. If she continues with this movement it may eventually, with practice, result in her walking - after a fashion. She has to try harder now that she is not playing with Angel all day and, as a result, she is bonding with us again and we are in a better position to help her. I just wish her teeth were not so sharp – she is like an alligator'. This prompted me to rename her the Maddiegator, as she was a little snapper!

I asked how Maddie spent her days, and Angie told me:

'Maddie has her own little routine: when I come down about 7:30 am, I open the cage door and say: 'Hi Maddie, do you want to get up yet?' Most days, Maddie yawns, stretches a leg out and goes straight back to sleep. This means 'hello, but I don't want to get up yet'. She doesn't usually get up until ten-thirty, does a wee on her paper, then eats her breakfast, plays with her toys and goes back to sleep on her pillow. She has a raw egg in the shell every day; most days she plays with it for ages before cracking it and eating it, but when she is in a mood she will just smack it straight away. When she finally gets up she might go out in the garden on her wheels or play with Angel for a while. This is repeated for the rest of the day till Harry comes home, when she gets really excited. She runs around the room like a whirlwind, which is her way of saying 'it's nice to see you'. She does the same when I have been busy in different rooms. When I come back to the breakfast kitchen Maddie grabs her ball and runs around like a cat having a mad half an hour, she wants me to throw the ball and clap my hands. When I stop clapping, Maddie stops dead and waits for me to start clapping again; then off she goes as before. Sometimes she grabs the feather duster and when I say 'shake' she tries to kill it. Harry can't believe that she is reacting to what I am saying and that she knows her name. You should have seen the look on his face when he first realised this. She then sits next to him by his chair and they watch TV together. He also plays with her; I think the game is called 'shred my newspaper' or 'chew my Crocs'. When Harry shouts 'bed', Maddie runs straight into her cage and goes to bed. She likes anything she can trash and doesn't want to do anything that *you* want her to do – like have a bath, put her harness on or if you are trying to stop her from going the way she wants to go outside. Equally, she does not like being stopped from hanging off the curtains and she has now pulled half the curtain hooks off the rail by doing that. Stroking her when she does not want to be stroked or picking her up also results in biting - she only does what she wants to do, she is a proper princess and acts like a diva. I leave her out of her cage nearly the whole day; so she does her own thing. We use the dog gate to separate her from the dogs but they lie nose to nose sometimes and seem to like each other. They are not exactly friends though as she hisses at them. Maddie likes Oscar best. He is used to Scarlett so he certainly would not hurt Maddie on purpose' but he is a bit too big to play with her.'

During September, Madelon came back to stay again and I took her to visit Maddie and the other foxes. We warned her that Maddie would bite now. She was amazed at how big she had grown, although she was tiny in comparison to

Angel. They were both about six months now. Maddie, who was running around in the room, was sitting behind Madelon's chair, eyeing up her open handbag with the iPhone in it. Not much escaped Miss Maddie's notice. Madelon put her hand down to touch her and Maddie promptly bit her. Oh dear, well we did warn her.

I would have loved a cuddle with Maddie, but instead of trying to touch her I fed her a couple of pieces of the steak that I had brought for her. She took them nicely from me, ate the first piece then buried the second piece under the blanket in her cage. Even though she always had plenty of food, her instinct to stock her larder for a rainy day clearly remained intact, although I recently read that foxes also cache food to share with other foxes in the family. I know they do it to feed their cubs, as I have observed foxes do this in my own garden. I put the rest of the meat on a little plate on top of her cage, as she obviously was not that hungry.

When Angel was brought in he immediately sniffed out Maddie's buried treasure and ate it. She followed him everywhere. How tall he was and how agile in comparison to Maddie. When he found the rest of her steak, he just reached up to the top of her cage and grabbed it with her looking on; she did not seem to mind all that much. He even jumped on top of it to look for more. He was so big, yet so friendly, we were all able to hold him and have a cuddle – you had to catch him first though, but we usually left that job to Christian.

After lunch we went outside to sit in the enclosure with Darla and Angel whilst Maddie had a rest. We took a great many photographs and I made a little video of Angel doing foxy pounces whilst he played with Christian. The two silver foxes were hard to distinguish by now; had it not been for the little white star on his chest I would not have known who was who. They were so photogenic, posing on the roof of the Wendy house, going down the slide and playing with us and with their toys. It was such a fun afternoon: Angel drank Maggie's apple juice behind her back and whilst we turned to watch him, Darla found my glass of champagne, knocked it over and scented on it – charming!

We left for home again late afternoon so that I would be back in time for Molly's insulin injection at eight o'clock, and to feed my wild garden foxes, of whom there were three every night on my front lawn - my life was ruled by animals, or so it seemed.

Towards the end of September I received this message from Angie:

'Maddie stood up tonight on all four legs and took two tiny wobbly steps all on her own. It was so quick I had to look twice. Harry saw her too or I would have thought I was dreaming. You know how a baby stands up and takes its first steps – it was just like that. She got excited when I came into the kitchen where she was sitting in her cage with the door open, I rolled her big ball and then she stood right up, wobbled a bit and then took two little steps. It was so fast, I said to Harry 'did you see what I just saw?' he said 'yes, I did'. She is doing funny things all the time with her back and legs.'

Such wonderful news. I was sure this was only the beginning of a new phase in Maddie's rehabilitation and was convinced she would just get up and walk one day soon, and so was Angie. I thought that her internet fans would go mad when I told them about it and I looked for an especially nice photo to accompany the news. I was not disappointed. I received many emotional and supportive messages, she had so many followers by now, and she was fast becoming an internet sensation. And still there were people asking 'when will she be released?' and 'will she stay with you or go to a sanctuary?'

Angie told them: *'Maddie is part of our world, our family; this is her home, forever, no matter what. Even if she is a bad foxy girl when she bites, we will still love her and care for her. She is funny, she plays and in her own way, she loves us too. She moves so very fast on her bottom and this is why we have the wheels – she needs to be upright. The messages from her brain are still muddled, but we are seeing changes in her movement and she has done different things in the last two weeks, movements we have not seen before, so just maybe things are starting to return. We knew it would take a long time, perhaps months, but we're still hopeful'.* Maddie's back legs keep opening *wide and she is trying to stand so that should give her better balance. Harry says if she is going to walk it will just happen and Angie has seen it all before: dogs that are completely paralysed for 9-10 months and then, one day, just walk into the surgery.'*

Patience really is a beautiful virtue.

Chapter 14

Halloween

In October, another drama took place in the foxy household, not involving Maddie, thank goodness, but Scarlett. Scarlett had been given a raw chicken drumstick, and through the connecting gate Darla had tried to get it off her and had ended up biting Scarlett's front leg. Scarlett had been screaming and Christian had come running to investigate the problem. Coming upon the scene of the crime, all he had seen initially was a piece of raw bone, blood and bits of fur. For one terrible moment he had thought that Darla had bitten Scarlett's foot off and I think he nearly had a heart attack with the shock of it. It turned out to be a deep flesh wound, almost down to the bone, and Scarlett had to be taken to the surgery to be stitched up and have antibiotics and painkillers. She then had to wear a cone until her leg was healed, poor girl; she was feeling very sorry for herself.

After this event the bottom half of the gate was obstructed so Darla could not get to her again. Darla and Scarlett had to be separated all the time now - could it be that Scarlett was jealous of Darla's babies? It was not quite what we had envisaged. Ideally, Scarlett would have 'adopted' Maddie, and Darla Angel, so that they would have had one each of their own kind – but that didn't happen, Darla protected both the cubs. It would have been so wonderful if they had all been friends and had played together in the double enclosure. As a result, Angie decided to extend Scarlett's enclosure so she would have a bigger space too. Christian had to set to work once more! It is now 17 feet by 20 feet.

During the half-term holiday, I visited again, this time with my granddaughter Emma. As it was around Halloween we brought some orange and black balloons, little oat cookies, cupcakes with witches on, a big chicken, and a play tent for Maddie. I was not sure how long the latter would last, but it would be fun for a bit to see her in it. Emma blew the balloons up and set up the play tent. As expected, the balloons did not last very long; they popped when Maddie tried to pick them up and she barely batted an eyelid at the noise. Christian said if that had been Scarlett she would have been a nervous wreck and would have hidden in the furthest corner of the house.

Not so Maddie – she was hard. She was in a great mood and sniffed out the little cookies in Emma's handbag straight away. Emma fed her some and played with her with a ball of paper. She was in and out of the tent, and so was Angel when he came in. Maddie stole one of Emma's boots and started chewing it behind a chair, thinking we would not notice perhaps. We had to watch her all the time, as per usual. However, 'Miss Bite' did not bite us and Angie thinks that Christian was right in separating Angel and Maddie for most of the day, as Maddie was trying harder and seemed to be bonding with her humans again. Angie said Maddie seemed to be mellowing, as she had not bitten her since August and she had also let Angie stroke her ears and legs occasionally - hurray!

Every now and then that afternoon, one of the ponies passed by the lounge and stared at us through the windows, which was so funny; the garden had been fenced off and they were both out of their field - 'mowing the lawn'. We went outside and fed them some apples and stroked their soft noses. Emma loves all animals, she wants to be a vet and I wish she would hurry up – we could do with one in my family. After we had given Angel a cuddle and before we left, Oscar came in and tried to sit on Emma's lap. She nearly disappeared underneath all that fur - he appeared even bigger than last time I had seen him.

Because Maddie now had her own 'castle' I called her 'HRH Princess Maddie of Cambridgeshire' but a princess she was not. HRH was a one-fox demolition squad, and the curtains in the breakfast room finally had to be taken down altogether when she managed to climb five feet up in them and pulled them down. Everything had fallen down on top of her, curtains, poles and a big glass vase, which miraculously had not broken. Angie admitted defeat and took the curtains down permanently. That night, Maddie had also shredded another bag of newspapers, and it took Angie till 5 am to clear up the mess, Maddie just ran into her cage when she saw Angie – she knew she had been a bad girl. What a little witch! It was all Harry's fault really, as he had forgotten to lock her cage after she had gone to bed. Because of the noise downstairs, Angie had gone to check on her at 2 am, but by then the damage had been done. The expensive curtains were put into storage.

There was another fall-out when Angie wanted to take a photo of her with the iPad, and HRH got really huffy because *she* couldn't have it. Bless her, she probably wanted to send me a selfie. The next night she got hold of Angie's feather quilt and ripped a hole in it. The feathers were everywhere, and Maddie had more feathers on her than the macaw. Now how did she get hold of that? She must have *stood up* to reach it as it was hanging up to dry.

Maddie liked to be clean, and every day she was given a fresh vet bed for her cage; it was nice and warm straight out of the tumble dryer and she buried herself in it straightaway. She dragged the cat bed into her room and slept in that. As for her mobilising, she would take three or four steps every now and then. She rolled along on her wheels, bunny hopped with her back legs crossed and climbed. Climbing was her favourite thing, along with swinging off any remaining curtains. She would climb up on the outside of her cage and grab things.

Maddie's play tent lasted six weeks before she trashed it and turned it into a play mat. She had seemed to like it however, and when Angie had put it in her room she had slept in it on her cushion and hidden her food in it. Maybe I can repair it next time I see her. Typical foxy behaviour: they have something for weeks, and then all of a sudden they wreck it.

Angel was nearly eight months now and had started to scent everywhere, even on Maddie, so on the 13th of November, Angel was neutered and Darla was spayed. Darla was twenty months old. Good-natured as he was, Angel made no fuss at all, not a sound, but Darla kicked off before she even saw the vet. She must have known where she was going, which made Angie think that her previous owners could have tried to get her spayed when she was younger and maybe the vet had refused to do it.

Darla went mad in the clinic. She was biting Christian and was 'as evil as they come before anyone had even touched her – biting much worse than Maddie', to use Angie's words, and she caused Christian much stress. Angie was just about ready to take her home again when Christian managed to get hold of her somehow. Anaesthetics are always risky and both Angie and he had been nervous about the procedures and were glad when it all went without a hitch in the end and the two foxes were safely home again. What a relief, and what a stressful day.

Three days later Darla was still very bad-tempered with Christian, so she had to wear her 'cone' longer than Angel; Angie said if she had taken it off too soon she would never have got it back on again. After the fight at the clinic with Christian, Darla hated Christian with a passion and kept going for him, but with Angie she was sort of OK. Poor Christian could not win, first Maddie turned her back on him and now Darla. Even when foxes are neutered or spayed, they can become moody and difficult during breeding time, and it was now November.

During November, Maddie kept teasing us; she was standing up on all fours, taking some steps, bucking with her back legs, rolling along on her wheels and moving her bad leg forward a little, following the front leg as would have been normal. Why would she not walk, because all this meant she could? It was a rollercoaster of emotions, two steps forward - one step back and vice versa.

CHAPTER 15

The Christmas Party

On December the 10th we celebrated Christmas early when Maggie and I were invited to come and see the foxes again. It would be Maddie's and Angel's first Christmas and it would be exciting to see them under the Christmas tree, or perhaps *in* the Christmas tree? You never know with foxes.

The journey up there was not too bad traffic wise, but it is still a long way and I arrived just after one o'clock. Maggie was already present and was sitting on the floor, camera at the ready. The lounge looked lovely and the tree was huge, reaching right up to the ceiling and even bending over a bit at the top; it looked very festive, decorated as it was with many foxy ornaments, baubles and tinsel. For obvious reasons the bottom branches had not been attached to the tree and the coloured lights in it were not on. Well, I have already told you how Scarlett had fused all the lights in the house when she was little; we did not want a repeat performance. Foxes are very fond of pulling and chewing wires. The fireplace was decorated too with branches and tinsel.

Maddie was in her cage in the room, dozing. She looked up when I came in and her ears went back for a minute or so. Whoa – a stranger! Fresh and fragrant from her bath that morning, she looked stunning with her glossy fur. When I told her how beautiful she looked she wore an expression as if to say 'I'm so worth it' to quote the L'Oreal adverts.

'Hello, Maddie darling' I said, 'say hello to your other mummy'. She came to the edge of the cage, sniffed my hand through the bars, and gave me a few little nips on my knuckles. I could not call it proper biting; I would like to think it was more of a love bite. After that she seemed fine and continued her chillaxing. Angie said that she had been running around all morning. I gave her a tiny oat cookie, which she took from me and immediately buried under her vet bed – some things never change.

There were presents for everyone, including all the animals, and over coffee we all decided we would like to open ours before we let Maddie out, as she seemed quite happy just resting for a while. Surprise, surprise, many of the presents were fox-themed, which made us all laugh; I think we had all been trying to find different fox-themed things in the shops and on-line. I had decided to adopt a donkey for Angie, because it would make a change for her to have an animal that she would not have to look after herself; she has enough to do with the ones she has already there, remember: five foxes, seven dogs, two ponies, five cats, some chickens and Mac the macaw. *Five* foxes? Oh yes, there are five now - I'll come to that in a minute.

After exchanging the presents and our news, we decided to have lunch in the dining room before we let the foxes out. There were scrumptious cakes for dessert, which we took back to the lounge. Then we let Maddie out and the fun began. She dashed around the room like a whirlwind, diving beneath sofas, hiding behind chairs and curtains. She seemed to be more upright than the last time I had seen her and I thought I noticed her using one of her back legs normally every now and then. Getting a decent photograph of her posing nicely by the tree was like 'Mission Impossible' of course, although if I possessed the skills and Photoshop I might have been able to cobble together one entire Maddie fox from the bits of her I managed to photograph: an ear, an eye, bit of tail, a paw, her back, her nose - anything but the entire Maddie sitting attractively with a Santa hat on and smiling! It was very funny.

I gave her a present and she ran away with it to hide it. Naturally we retrieved it and she did it again and again, even pulling the ribbon as though she was going to open it.

I took one of the cooked chicken legs which I had bought off the bone and called her over. She came to me and I was able to hand-feed her a few bits, although she did not seem very hungry. Angie said she had eaten a huge raw drumstick a couple of hours earlier, so it was not surprising. It was lovely to have her come so close. However I was feeding slippery, greasy chicken pieces with one hand and holding the bone in the other, so I could not take a picture of her close to me. I was not even sure if Maggie managed one, and she is a much better photographer than I am. I put the rest of the chicken on a plate on the floor in front of me, hoping Maddie would be back, but she chose to ignore it.

She played with the Santa hat, stuck her nose in it, and carried it around; at one stage we had a tug-of war with it when I put my hand in it and shook the white bobble on the top at her and she tried to get it off me. I loved playing with her. I even managed to touch her tail and back when her attention was on something else – her fur felt very soft, and I don't think she even noticed I did it. She was so excited. But her excitement was nothing compared to that when Christian brought Angel in; we all knew how fond they were of each other, and when he came into the room carrying the big black silver fox, you should have seen the change in Maddie. She danced around him, mouth open, panting and smiling – there was her big beautiful friend! She tried to stand up and reach him, but all she managed to do was to get his tail in her mouth. You could see her thinking 'put him down, put him down, I want to play with my friend, let me get to him!'

Christian put Angel on the floor. He immediately sussed out the chicken on the plate in front of me and ate some pieces, thereby prompting Maddie to want some more too. She bumped him out of the way and ate some of the chicken. He sat on her and ate some more and there was a general pushing and shoving between them until it was all gone. I took another drumstick, said 'SIT' and they sat in front of me like a pair of puppies whilst I tore off the meat; they took it from my hand in turn. The fun ended with Angel stealing the bone out of my hand, which he is not allowed to have of course as it was a cooked bone; he ran off with it, but Christian chased him and retrieved it before he could eat it, thank goodness. Like dogs, foxes must not have cooked chicken bones, as they can splinter and pierce their intestines. Angel then got a whiff of our cake and started climbing on the furniture to reach it, so we moved the cake on top of the cage - not that this action stopped him, he still managed to lick some of the icing off.

Although they were now both supposed to be fully-grown foxes at nine months of age, Maddie seemed tiny compared to Angel. Obviously, because he is a male it makes a difference, but once again all of us were 100% convinced that she had been the runt of a litter. They both disappeared under the tree and were without doubt considering pulling the tinsel down from the bottom of the tree when Maddie took a red glass bauble in her mouth instead. We shouted 'NO' at her and she let go immediately, so we swiftly moved it higher up. She does seem to know what 'no' means.

The thing is whilst you are watching one fox the other one is up to something, they are so fast; I suddenly noticed Maddie was under the sofa with the bag of *my* presents which she had pulled down. I had to crawl down under the sofa to get them back and afterwards I lay down on the rug wondering what the foxes would do now. Angel ignored me, but Maddie treated me as an obstacle course and clambered all over me whilst continuing to run about chasing Angel. I could feel some sniffing and tugging on my hair.

'Is there an animal pulling my hair?' I asked.

'Yes there is,' came the reply.

'What colour is it, red or black?'

'Red.'

I might have known it; Maddie was pulling my hair. I distracted her by putting my hand under the rug and scratching it, which made her abandon my hair in order to come over to see what was under the rug. Not finding a rat, she soon moved on to investigate the pile of discarded wrapping paper by the fireplace and started to run about with the Santa hat and one of the unopened foxy presents. She even got hold of a scented candle and sniffed it with great interest. During the rest of the afternoon, Angie's tidy lounge was gradually transformed into a mess of discarded wrapping paper, ribbons, crumbled cookies, shredded chews and toys, with people and foxes crawling about and running around in it. What a fantastic party.

By now it was already dark outside and quite cold too, so we did not go out to see the other *three* foxes in their pens. Yes, three - a fifth fox had been adopted, Lewie, a wild red fox approximately the same age as Scarlett. He had been rescued suffering from mange and toxoplasmosis, which had left him with some brain damage. He had arrived at Angie's house via the National Fox Welfare Society, where he had been treated, and although he was now no longer a danger to other foxes with regard to infection, he could not go back to the wild and they had been looking for a safe forever home. Angie offered to have him as a possible companion for Scarlett, so now she had five foxes: Scarlett, Darla, Maddie, Angel and Lewie.

Toxoplasmosis is a parasitic disease which infects the part of the brain that is usually associated with fear and the fight or flight instinct. Symptoms noticed in toxo-positive foxes are as follows: no fear and no real signs of aggression, circling, head-pressing and food dangling from the fox's mouth whilst the fox seems completely unaware of this. Walking up to an object and then just standing there, seemingly unaware of the fact that if it moved to the left or right it could pass the object in the way. Following feet but unaware of things going on above knee level, teeth grinding, and in extreme cases, fitting.

Whilst the fox can't pass on this disease, it is left with the condition none the less. However some foxes in good health and with a good immune system can fight this successfully. The National Fox Welfare Society has treated many toxo-infected foxes over the years, however none have been suitable for release back to the wild as the condition leaves them almost like domestic dogs.

After they were slowly introduced to each other over several weeks, Scarlett had a wild red companion after all, a big male this time. Lewie was not ready for visitors yet when we were there, so I did not see him, and after another mug of tea and a mince pie 'for the road', Maggie and I left. I always found it hard to leave Maddie and just wanted to take her with me; she would easily have fitted into my bag. I must admit that I felt quite envious of her interaction with her carers – would I ever get a cuddle with my rescued baby again? I guess not. As compensation, Oscar leant over the gate and licked me goodbye.

During December the bond between Maddie and her vet grew stronger. She seemed to love him. She was always very excited when he arrived home at night, and she still watched TV with him, sitting at his feet or *on* his feet like a puppy; occasionally she bit him. He thought she was quite amazing. And to think he used to hunt foxes when he was a young man of about nineteen. I wonder if he ever thinks about that these days.

Shortly after our visit, Angel spent a day in London. Not surprisingly, given his good looks and good nature, he had been chosen to be the face of an anti-fur campaign by Angels of the Innocent Foundation - (I prefer my fox with a heartbeat) - so Christian and Angie had to take him to London for the day for a photo shoot. He lived up to his name the photo and the video turned out beautiful. He did not even need any make-up. He is such a lovely boy. You can see the campaign video with Angel and Anneka Svenska on this Facebook page: www.facebook.com/AngelsfortheInnocent/videos. Just watch Anneka, Christian and Angel and then tell me how one could ever justify stripping his skin off and wearing him as a coat. I know I also prefer my coat with a heartbeat - I have always known.

Maddie, who had to stay home, was delighted to see Angie back and greeted her very enthusiastically by running around, pulling her hair and bringing Angie her toys. So was Scarlett, who kept grabbing Angie's hand and running round just like a cub – how lovely to think they had missed her. The next day it was pay-back time and Maddie helped Angie to *untidy* the kitchen; she got the mop out of the bucket and made a terrible mess.

Christmas Day was full of fun; Maddie and all the other foxes had been spoilt by Santa and they played with their new toys. They had cake and ice cream too – foxes do like a chunk of jammy Swiss roll. For Maddie though, the best part of the day was ripping off labels, ribbons and shredding wrapping paper; mind you, that was nothing new really, as all Maddie's days were like Christmas Day.

Chapter 16

Happy New Year

January brought storms and rains, which made the foxes moody; they did not like the high winds, and hid in their beds. They did not want to get up and on some days were all nipping, not in a nasty way – more in a naughty way. Angie thought it might be due to the fact that January is the breeding season, so it could be that they were playing up because of their hormones.

Angie wanted to get Maddie swimming to strengthen her legs, but the garden was flooded and she could not fill the bath up full as the drainage tank in the garden would have overflowed. Maddie had a little life jacket, and I would have so loved to have seen her in it, but one after another everybody, including me, caught a virus and suffered flu, coughs and colds. We felt awful, so I did not see her that month. On the better days when Maddie was in a good mood, she would run around all day playing with a dog sausage – goodness only knows why.

One day, when Angie took Maddie out on her wheels, she took off like a rocket after Lizzy, the ginger cat. She chased after her so fast that she turned her wheels over on their side, which quite shocked her - I believe the cat was quite shocked too. Maddie had to have her lead back on to keep an element of control and to stop her disappearing into the hedge. I asked Angie if she thought she would ever walk, but she was not sure now. Angie said that there would definitely be more of a chance if she did not bite so much when they wanted to help her. But we already know that Maddie did not do anything that she did not want to do. She was a very independent little fox. If she could not have her own way she would bite as she did me, Madelon, another friend and, unsurprisingly, Christian, Harry and Angie many times.

'She is lovely and you can hand feed her and play with her but if you try to touch her she will bite you' said Angie. 'Sometimes she will let you stroke her but she is so fast you really have to watch out and it is not just a nip either, it is a full crunch.' Accordingly I renamed her 'Her Royal Biteness Maddie of Cambridge'. I enjoyed thinking up silly names for her, if only to amuse her fans.

As if to prove us all wrong, Maddie now started to stand up on four legs, leaning on the freezer and taking some little steps. She resembled a baby about to walk but unable to, or unwilling to. Besides, Maddie moved so fast on her bottom that we thought perhaps she could not be bothered. Why should she? She was very happy doing her bum shuffle as babies do, and she could easily keep up with Angel. With her so small and him so big we really needed a miracle or even half of one because there was no reason for her not to walk, apart from the fact that the messages from brain to legs had not quite sorted themselves out yet. She had no spinal injury so we still lived in hope.

Maddie found another way of mobilising when she was given a Frisbee; she did not use it to throw around – no, she sat on it and treated it like a skateboard, pushing with her back legs to get it moving around the floor and thereby making a great deal of noise. It was yet another way of using her legs. We kept our fingers crossed. Angie started to play even more with her, holding things up and trying to get her to reach for them by shouting 'up, up, Maddie', anything to encourage her to stand up properly.

Then, in the first week in February, we had some snow. Angie put Maddie outside and she sat there in the snow and sat properly with her legs tucked under her. It was lovely to see. Angie did not want her to get cold, so she was not out that long, but Maddie must have been preoccupied with all that white stuff because she completely forgot to bite Angie when she picked her up to bring her in again. To make up for that oversight, she bit her for no reason at all when

Angie changed the water bowl in her room. Haha! Can you believe it? What a naughty minx. I suggested putting her back in the snow on her bottom to cool off, then, when she got really cold, she might stand up, but Angie would not risk that.

Everyone in the Evans household caught bugs, flu and chest infections in turn - for the second time - and as if that was not enough bad luck, Mac the macaw suddenly died. Christian had cleaned his cage and he was fine, yet an hour later Angie found him lying dead at the bottom of his cage. She was very shocked; he had been with her for eighteen years. She estimated him to be probably about forty years old. It was nothing to do with Maddie, thank goodness; it looked as if he had had a heart attack. We thought Maddie would be lost without his company and his 'hello' chattering, but Maddie now struck a deal with the dogs, or so it seemed; they got her vet bed under the gate and she got their dog biscuits in return, what a funny girl. She also kept lying together with Oscar by the baby gate and Angie was going to try them together for a short while. He would be the best dog to be her friend because he was brought up with Scarlett and is used to foxes. If it worked out and he was not too rough with her they could eventually sleep together. However when she tried this experiment, Maddie growled and barked at Oscar. It was such a shame, as she would have had a nice new companion. Because Angie had been taken ill during February she had not been able to play ball with Maddie in the mornings the way she used to, which did not please Miss Maddie. She even growled at Angie when she did manage to go down and see her.

As I had estimated Maddie's age at six weeks when I found her, we celebrated her first birthday on the 16th of March 2015. Like the Queen she had two birthdays as Angie thought it might have been a bit later, the 20th. She will have been with the Evans family for a year by the 30th of April. We do not know what happened to Maddie at the beginning of this story and we can only guess how it will end. I would love to say, 'she stood up and started to walk', but I can't. We know this much: when Maddie came to Angie's family her legs were totally dead, which was the reason for getting Angel. With all the work they did on her, and through playing with Angel her legs started to move. At first we thought it was just a nerve reaction but no; Maddie started to move her legs because she wanted to play with her new little friend.

She may walk yet, and there have been plenty of times when we all thought she would. Especially in November 2014, when her demeanour changed to being a nice girl again the same as she was when she was a baby. She let Angie stroke her head and ears and her legs occasionally. It was the first time she had let Angie do that since she had grown up, so maybe be we did have a bit of the crazies early. She did not bite unless Angie tried to pick her up. She played with Angie's hair and she smiled at her with a softer look in her eyes, as Scarlett does. Several times she stood up and took some steps, which was a first since she grew up.

Possibly, had there not been so much illness in February, Maddie's routine would not have been disrupted. She was also becoming a bit wary of strangers, just like Scarlett. Now that Maddie is 'grown up' she no longer plays with Darla, as Angie does not trust Darla after her attacks on Scarlett – you never know. Mind you, 'grown up'? Yes in age, but not in stature: she's a mini fox. Yet Maddie is not thin, she is just right and has the elegant long legs of an adult vixen, albeit a very small one.

CHAPTER 17

Being a diva

Many people wanted to bring their pet foxes to play with Angie's foxes. However foxes are not like dogs; most dogs are happy to play together, even if they don't know each other – not so foxes. Moreover, Angie's foxes have each other: Scarlett has the company of Lewie, who is easy and happy and potters around in the enclosure with Scarlett - she can handle him and they now sleep together in the kennel. He is coming on fine and is regaining some of his brain functions. Darla is fine with Angel. Maddie plays with Angel, but all he wants to do these days is get in her crate to see if she has hidden any food in there before going to sleep in it – no, not in the food, he eats that, in her crate of course.

It is now April, and Maddie continues to stand up nearly

every day, but she just does not walk. She gets moody when the cleaner goes into her room and takes it out on Angie and Harry by growling at them. She definitely does not like to have her routine upset – don't even think of moving her crate to the other side of the room, as Christian did recently. She was sulking and growling at everyone till Angie moved it back to its original place.

Maddie says:

'It is my room, my crate, my cushion, and my vet bed by the glass doors. You are going into my home when you enter it. I do not like to be moved, only to play with Angel and that has to be in the lounge as he jumps up too high now to play in the kitchen – there are cookers, hobs and other things that he could hurt himself on or that could be broken. As far as I am concerned, my room is safe: I never get hungry, I can play with my toys and watch the dogs when they are outside; I can watch TV, I can play ball with my human mummy or help her thrash the kitchen and get away with it. My vet sits with me at night and then I have a nice warm clean vet bed and a midnight snack to go to bed with. When I am told to go to bed, off I go. I don't wet my bed either; I get up in the morning and go on a newspaper. I am a good girl'.

Maddie is just over a year old now and has mellowed a little. Lacking curtains in her room, she now likes hanging off

Angie's long skirts and she has already bitten a big hole in the new cushion on Harry's chair. He was sitting on it and she wanted it, so she tugged and tugged until she got it. She has also been playing outside again with Angel, for short periods only, as he tends to be a little rough with her. Actually she bullies him too if the truth be known. She gets about so fast she knocks the scab off her leg every now and then and, as a result of this action, she has to wear a cone to aid healing, as she won't leave it alone. Without the cone on Maddie is like a child with a scab on its knee – she keeps picking at it - just a bad habit. Outside, Angel started to drag her around by that cone and Angie had to bring her in again resulting in a sulk. Many times I have offered to have Maddie back but Angie won't part with her, this is what she says:

'I would be lost without Maddie; we have a nice routine each morning. Whether she does walk, eventually, after a fashion, or whether she does not, it does not matter to me; she has fun playing, she eats well, she is happy and she is funny and she knows it. She is also very much loved, I can't imagine life without her. She is tiny so she will always be a baby, funny and cute as they come. She is her own boss and is a very proud girl. Even though I hand feed her every day and she likes to play she will only do what she wants to do.'

But we already knew that.

In other words, Angie, your little red patient is a diva, a tiny red diva. We all love you Maddie. Photos of you and your antics have brought so much pleasure to so many people world-wide. You have been an education and an inspiration for many people. On April 28th it was exactly a year since I found you, and rightly or wrongly I decided to save you. You are a brave girl and a real fighter, you are not scared of anything, especially not of people who turn up with treats for you, isn't that right?

This is not the end of Maddie's story though…

Chapter 18

Maddie falls in love!

During the first couple of weeks in April, Maddie had rearranged her room several times; the way she was moving everything around made me think she was now employed by Pickford's Removals. She moved her crate, her cushion, the stool, a chair, her bed and her toys all around the kitchen. She even moved the breeze blocks that were at the side of the cooker to stop her getting behind it - she's so strong. We wondered what she was up to.

During those two weeks, Maddie had also been introduced several times to Lewie and Scarlett outside. She loved it! Lewie, especially, followed her around everywhere and really seemed to like her; it was mutual. She seemed very excited in his presence, and even stood up properly and remained standing. When Angie took her back in, she threw a paddy and started trashing the kitchen. She clearly wanted to go back out. Now what was the matter with her?

A couple of days later Angie noticed some blood on the kitchen floor. Had Maddie hurt herself or – err - could it be.....? Despite a lot of protest, growling and hissing she was unceremoniously turned upside down by Christian and guess what had happened? She was on heat! Our little girl had become a woman. And we had been thinking that she would always be a baby.... yeah right!

Hence Lewie's interest in her - he must have known what was up! Obviously that part of his brain had not been affected by the toxoplasmosis. Clearly she had known as well; he is an entire male, the only one there, and maybe all the moving around had been her way of preparing a den. Bless her. Because of her size it had come as a bit of a surprise to us, and so late in the year as well. Foxes normally are in season in December/January.

Obviously she would not be able to go out to see Lewie now. It is a blessing foxes are only fertile for three days, because this hormonal woman was not best pleased at having her love life scuppered. She was seriously cheesed off with Angie, tried to bite her legs and her feet and tried to escape. She must have been so frustrated.

Don't get too excited though. There will not be any little Maddies or Lewies in the future - can you imagine what she would be like with cubs? She would be extremely protective and possessive. Moreover, what would we do with them? She could not rear them naturally in the wild and she probably would not let anyone near them. In any case it would be unethical to breed from a wild red fox, so that's definitely not happening.

Now that she has had her first season and we know that everything is in working order, so to speak, Angie is going to have her spayed. It might calm her down as it has Darla. Maddie has had an anaesthetic once before, so she should be all right.

On my recent visit Darla and Angel were playing together outside and when I went into their space to sit with them and to feed them some chicken, Darla was lovely. It might have had something to do with the two cooked chicken breasts I was holding, but they took turns trying to climb on my lap to be fed. At times, I even had both of them on my lap at the same time. Darla had never been like that on previous visits. Angel - our gentle playboy - yes, but not Darla. Oh, they both still nibbled my coat, pulled my hair, nipped at my shoes and stole my brooch, but Darla was very much calmer than I had ever seen her, so perhaps spaying Maddie will do the same for her - calm her down and stop her nipping so much. Let's hope so.

Having said that, a lovely thing happened when I was there that day: Maddie let me stroke her! She even half-closed her eyes and went all soppy on me. I spoke softly to her and said 'tickle, tickle, tickle', whilst I scrabbled my fingers in the soft fur on her back, as Angie does, and she stayed like that for ages by the side of my chair. Angie said she had been doing the same to her almost daily.

True, in order to stop Maddie picking at the scab on one of her legs, she was wearing a collar, so my fingers were not near her face and she could not whip her face around suddenly to bite me. I was relatively safe, but it made my day, as I had not expected that. She felt all soft and warm, and it was wonderful to touch her again.

For a belated birthday present I had brought her a child's pop-up play tunnel. Remember I have told you that foxes are frightened of anything new? Not Maddie. Without batting an eyelid she ran through it straightaway, and when Angie put it in her room later she started moving it about and positioning it exactly where she wanted it. I expect it will go the way of her 'castle' eventually, but for now she has something new to play with.

It has been a wonderful year with many adventures. You would not believe how fast Maddie moves, and whilst unfortunately, she does not seem to want to walk more than a few steps, we hope that a new rescued female companion due to arrive soon from the NFWS will give her the interaction with one of her own kind that she deserves. Angel is far too big for her now - he plays too rough. Maddie and her new friend will have a new enclosure built especially for them with smooth tiles on the floor, and I hope that all foxes will have a long and happy life with Angie.

I shall continue to visit them of course. How could I not?

CHAPTER 19

Think you want a pet fox?

Many people who have seen Maddie and Angel's photos and videos think it would be easy and fun to own a pet fox. Opinions on owning a fox as a pet vary, but generally speaking **wild** red foxes make bad pets unless they have been rescued as very small babies and have been hand-reared. Even then they can be unpredictable. Red foxes that cannot be released back to the wild often end up in a sanctuary.

Before acquiring any type of pet, you should do your research and fully understand what owning that species of animal requires of you. Food availability, finances, enclosures, safety, environment, and your schedule and availability should all affect this decision - alongside common sense.

I quote from the website of exotic pets expert Adrienne

Kruzer: 'Foxes, along with cats, are my favourite animals. Their depth and uniqueness appeal to me. Every fox is an individual character. Some are very elusive, while others can be quite friendly and cheeky. Some are very spontaneous and playful and some are just plain boring – in fact they are just like people'

Here are the pros and cons of owning a tame-bred pet fox, as I see them:

Pros:

- They are fascinating, but you must be consistent to earn their trust.
- They are playful and you can watch them all day.
- They are funny and cheeky and beautiful to see and they come in a range of colours
- They are quite independent so can be left for short periods. You can walk them on a lead.
- You can cuddle them like a puppy.
- They like to play with dogs and children.
- They will not eat your cat.
- Small pet foxes, like Fennecs, can live in your house all the time.

Cons:

- Unlike dogs, pet foxes lack the trait to want to please humans, so they do what they want.
- They need a large, secure, outdoor enclosure with a warm kennel and plenty of hiding and climbing places from about 5-6 months.

- They have a musky smell which, when mixed with water, is extremely powerful.

- They are hard to litter-train. Some will use a puppy pad, but generally they poo and pee and scent on everything they consider theirs, such as their bed, their food, toys and water bowls and you.

- They will jump, pounce and climb all over your house.

- They are more destructive than a puppy and will never grow up.

- They need a great deal of stimulation and entertainment.

- They can be very shy, mainly with strangers.

- They are scared of anything new.

- They require a great deal of time and patience.

- They love to dig, so they cannot go in a garden without a lead as they can jump 6 ft fences easily.

- They sulk if you upset them in any way, or if there is a change in routine.

- You should be 100% certain and do a lot of research before getting a pet fox, as they are hard to rehome, which is not fair on the animal.

- You must find a specialised vet before even considering getting a fox.

- The fox should, ideally, be neutered or spayed before its first mating season.

The friends I have got to know during this year who own pet foxes say that if you can hack the first six months, you're going to make it as a fox parent and I would agree with that.

My Little Red Patient was extremely lucky to end up living with Angie, Christian and Harry. All I did was to pick her up off the road that fateful night a year ago and refuse to have her put down. I hope others who find themselves in my position would have done the same, or at the very least have phoned for help from a wildlife rescue organisation, preferably not the RSPCA. Perhaps I can encourage you to put a phone number in your mobile phone now; there are some phone numbers on the contacts page.

Foxes have always been thought to be nocturnal and very shy animals. And indeed they often are. Not by nature, but because we gave them a reason to be - by hunting them, so to end this book, here is a poignant poem written for me by a friend.

The Fox's Lament

I'm sly and cunning, you don't trust in me.
I stalk and torment, that's all you see.
You don't come near, because you fear
The wolf in rusty clothing - such tales!
It seems that superstition prevails.

I glare and I most fiercely glower,
Staring at prey with evil power.
Skulking at night, I snarl and bite.
Stealing, hunting, killing for sport,
And wilfully cruel? So it is thought.

I'm sadly misunderstood, I cry,
And so hated without knowing why.
No lion's maw - a narrow jaw,
Furry and cute and cheerfully red
Still doesn't stop you from wanting me dead.

But I exist, I endure, I live
With a tenacity you can't forgive.
You judge, refute and persecute,
And when I am trapped and waiting to die,
You can't even look me in the eye.

You hold court over my life and ways,
Condemning my home, the broods I raise.
Pretty painted, real life tainted.
You stalk; you torment and hunt to kill,
Loathing the fact that I remain, still.

You think I'm bad, but why is it good
To concrete my field, chop down my wood,
Destroy our lands with selfish hands?
Whatever I am, whatever I do,
None on earth are as wicked as you.

And when you have wiped the animals out
You can stand and gaze at all about
No furry thing, nor bird on wing
Shall wander around this common place
And your sorrow shall wear a vulpine face.

Mary Page, 2014

Epilogue

✚

During the first week in June I went to stay with Angie for a few days. Christian was on holidays and I went to help look after the foxes, except Scarlett and Lewie; Scarlett ran and hid as soon as she heard my voice. I enjoyed the interaction with Angel and Darla and tidied up their enclosure. Darla tried her very best to grab my camera and to nip me every time I was in there but Angel was his usual sweet self.

They were so gentle when I gave them their treats. All the foxes looked a bit scruffy as they were now shedding their winter coats, which caused them to have a good scratch every now and then. There was fur everywhere - if only they had stood still for a minute so that we could have given them a good brushing, but they were always running about. Just their tails remained as magnificent as ever.

The highlight of this week was playing with Maddie and sitting with her in her room. She was adorable - and she no longer bites. She has grown up and has learned to trust her human family. I think she has realised which side her bread is buttered. Instead of biting she let me stroke her, put her wet nose on my hand and sniffed to see if I had any treats. She's a lovely clean girl and likes her clean vet bed at least twice a day. Mind you, she peed on the floor as soon as I had washed it; she obviously preferred her own scent.

I had to take great care not to leave my laptop lead or my handbag within reaching distance, as she didn't miss a trick and would have pulled them down. Once or twice I forgot to close the dog gate and she went straight out into the kitchen. It's difficult enough to prepare food with three Westies under my feet, but with Maddie trying to get to them it was downright impossible. You have to realise that I am not used to having so many animals around me in the kitchen, so when I said they were under my feet I meant literally *under* my feet as I clumsily managed to stand on a tail here and a paw there. I even stood on one of the hens' feet when I went outside to collect the eggs. Poor Angie nearly had four disabled animals instead of just the one, but fortunately no animals were hurt during my visit.

The new football I had brought for Maddie lasted about ten minutes before she bit through it and deflated it – note to self: buy sturdier toys for her. It surprised me to see that she still had her birthday present in one piece, the play tunnel. At times she resembled a snail with its shell on top as she scooted around the room wearing the tunnel. It was comical to watch.

I talked to her all the time, called her 'my princess' and hand-fed her pieces of steak or chicken. We watched the dogs together through the window and we could also see Lewie walking around. Angie and I sat with her during the day till she fell asleep, and then again kept her company in the evenings. She seemed to take several naps each day. I'd like to think she enjoyed our company.

Angel was now too big to play with her apart from very short periods, so Angie was arranging to buy a small tame cub as a playmate for Maddie; we waited anxiously to hear when it would arrive.

Two days after I went home Lewie suddenly became very ill. He was rushed to the clinic and put on a drip. Suffering acute kidney failure, he passed away the next day. It seemed the toxoplasmosis had affected other organs besides his brain, which happens sometimes. Still, it came as a real shock as he had been fine all week; he had played about his enclosure with Scarlett and had eaten well. After eight months of his company Scarlett was now on her own again. It was such a shame as Lewie and she had been getting on well, not to mention the fact that he had been Maddie's love interest.

Shortly after this sad episode the new cub arrived, a tame eight-week-old calico fox. He was an amazing colour with white spotty feet, black socks, brown flanks and a white stripe down the middle of his face. He was put in a crate in Maddie's room by way of introduction. She became super excited and as always when she's excited, she stood up. He put his paws through the bar and she did not bite him, so he was let out into her room. She loved him instantly but was a bit rough with him; she chased him down the play tunnel, pinned him down and pulled his legs till he squealed. Suddenly Maddie-the-mini-fox now looked enormous next to the baby, who seemed to prefer Angie's company - and who can blame him!

The new gentle boy was given the name Byron, after Lord Byron the poet, who was a great animal lover and had many animals as pets during his lifetime including a fox. The name suits him well. In a couple of weeks he will have grown and will be better at coping with his boisterous companion. For now he's allowed to be a baby.

The dynamics in Maddieland (as I call it) seem to change continuously, Angie will try Byron with Scarlett and Maddie with Darla and Angel to find the best way forward for our little disabled fox. Maddie is getting fitter every day and is building up the muscles in her legs. As soon as the new outdoor enclosure with a smooth floor for her has been finished, she will have more play time outside with her companions and Angie can have her breakfast room back.

For now all is well with this interesting and fascinating fox family.

Further Reading

The Little Red Thief, Louise Wren (2014)

Free Spirit – a brush with a fox, Michael Chambers (1990)

Urban Foxes, second edition, Stephen Harris and Phil Baker (2001)

Fox Watching, second edition, Martin Hemmington (2014)

USEFUL CONTACTS (find them on Facebook)

National Fox Welfare Society – www.nfws.org.uk
01933 411996 - 24hr recue 0778 183954

The Fox Man – Freshfields Animal Rescue (nr.Liverpool)
www.freshfieldsrescue.org.uk - 24hr rescue - 0151 931 1604

East Sussex WRAS Wildlife Rescue & Ambulance Service
24hr rescue - 07815 078 234

Burton Wildlife Rescue and Linjoy Sanctuary (Midlands)
24hr rescue - 07780742748

Selby Wildlife Rescue - www.selbywildlife.co.uk
07803 183 720 - North Yorkshire

Riverside Wildlife Rescue
www.riversideanimalcentre.org London

The Fox Project – www.foxproject.org.uk 01892 824111
wildlife ambulance service 9-9pm Kent

Hart Wildlife Rescue - 9-5pm - 09135 800 001
Hampshire - www.hartwildlife.org.uk

South Essex Wildlife Hospital
www.southessexwildlife.org.uk 01375 893893

Wildlife Aid Foundation – www.wildlifeaid.org.uk
24hr rescue - 09061 800 132 - Surrey

Kays Hill Sanctuary, Rescue Centres County Durham,
www.KaysHillsanctuary, www.rescue-centres.co.uk/animal-rescue-
centres-county%20durham-C12 Co Durham

www.helpwildlife.co.uk - to find the nearest wildlife
rescue in your area

Secret World Wildlife Rescue, Somerset
www.secretworld.org/inex.html

Fox-A-Gon - www.fox-a-gon.co.uk

Others can be found by typing the words 'wildlife rescue' plus the
name of your area or town into your search engine.